Edinburgh

A New History

The endpapers are taken from an 1804 map by John Ainslie, showing part of the Old Town (front) and the New Town (back) just before its second major expansion (Trustees of the National Library of Scotland)

Edinburgh

A New History

ALISTAIR MOFFAT

BIRLINN

First published in 2024 by
Birlinn Limited
West Newington House
10 Newington Road
Edinburgh
EH9 1QS

www.birlinn.co.uk

ISBN: 978 1 78027 905 3

British Library Cataloguing-in-Publication Data
A catalogue record for this book is available from the British Library

Typeset by Hewer Text UK Ltd, Edinburgh
Map by Helen Stirling

Papers used by Birlinn Ltd are from well-managed
forests and other responsible sources

Printed and bound by Clays Ltd, Elcograf S.p.A.

For Sandy McCall Smith

Contents

Contents

Foreword

Edinburgh has selected 2024 to mark the start of the 900th anniversary of our city. It was at this time that King David I founded Edinburgh as a royal burgh, marking the beginnings of self-governance for a small hilltop settlement that was to become the thriving capital city it is today.

The city's past means many things to many people. For some, it's a city of medieval kingship, faith, ideas, celebration and commerce; for others, a place of industry, conflict, leisure, finance and diversity. This book recognises these themes and so much more. It takes us on a journey from Edinburgh's glacial beginnings and prehistoric past through major events, such as the Reformation, the Enlightenment and the establishment of the world's greatest festival of the arts, until we arrive at today's modern metropolis.

Focusing on individuals, events and places, Alistair Moffat skilfully tells Edinburgh's many stories in an exciting and accessible way. He does not, however, shy away from the more challenging and darker aspects of Edinburgh's past, including the city's links to witchcraft and slavery. He provides a timely reminder that we must continue to learn from our past to shape a better future.

The book demonstrates that, through the efforts of its merchants, trades and citizens of all faiths and backgrounds, Edinburgh has grown to become a modern, vibrant and inclusive city.

As we look to its future, this new history is a testament to the efforts of those who have gone before, and a timely reminder of what can be achieved locally, nationally and internationally through the united efforts of all Edinburghers.

Robert Aldridge
The Rt Hon. Lord Provost of the City of Edinburgh

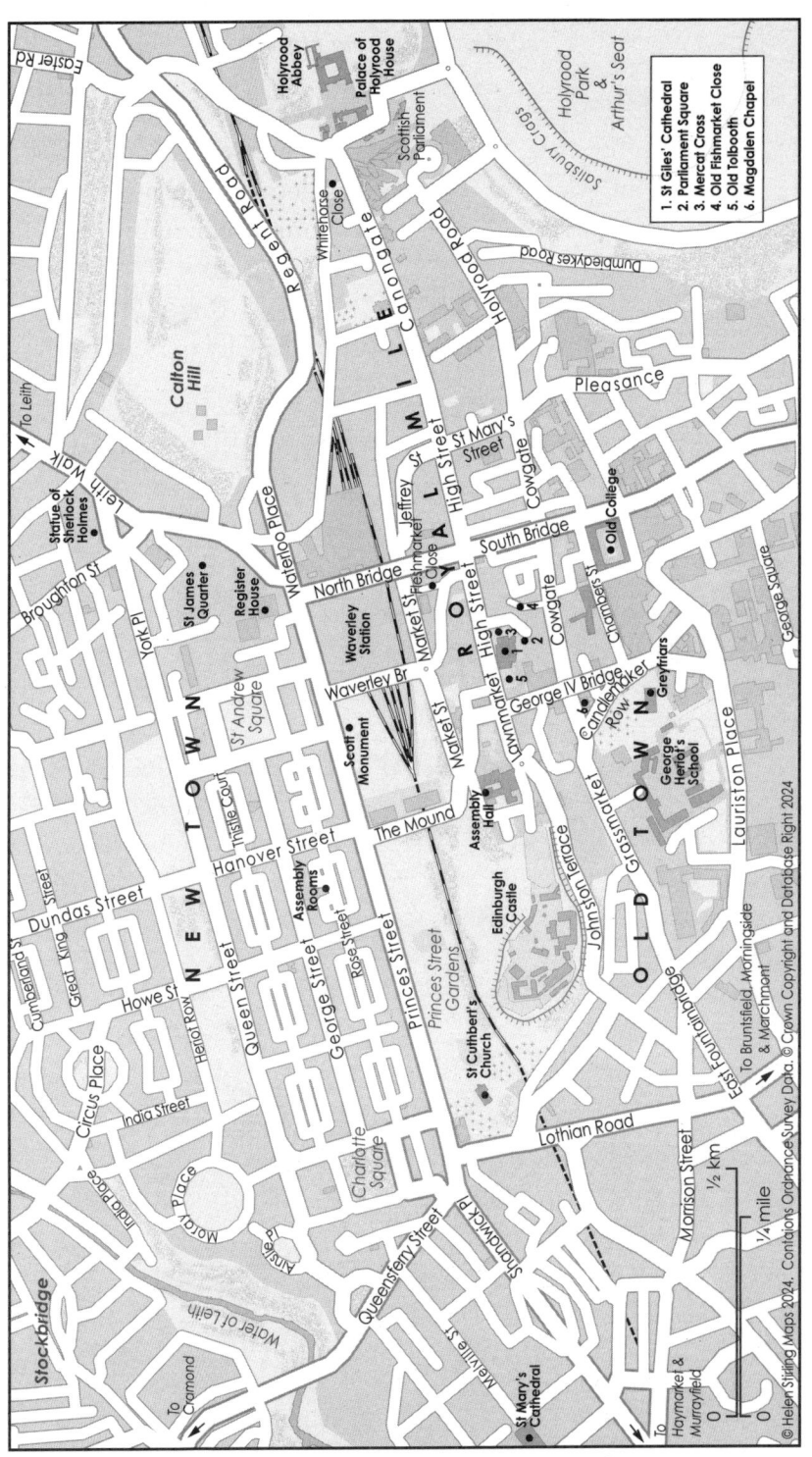

Key:
1. St Giles' Cathedral
2. Parliament Square
3. Mercat Cross
4. Old Fishmarket Close
5. Old Tolbooth
6. Magdalen Chapel

Areas and landmarks:

Stockbridge

To Cramond
To Leith

Statue of Sherlock Holmes
Broughton St
York Pl
St James Quarter
Register House
St Andrew Square
Thistle Court
Hanover Street
Assembly Rooms
George Street
Rose Street
Queen Street
Heriot Row
Howe St
Dundas Street
Great King Street
Cumberland St
Circus Place
India Street

NEW TOWN

Water of Leith
Ainslie Pl
India Place
Moray Place
Charlotte Square
Queensferry Street
Shandwick Pl
Melville St
St Mary's Cathedral

To Haymarket & Murrayfield

Morrison Street
Lothian Road
East Fountainbridge
To Brunsfield, Morningside & Marchmont

Princes Street
Princes Street Gardens
St Cuthbert's Church
The Mound
Waverley Br
Scott Monument
Waverley Station
North Bridge
Market St
Fleshmarket Close
Jeffrey St

Edinburgh Castle
Johnston Terrace
Assembly Hall
Lawnmarket
The Mound

OLD TOWN

George IV Bridge
Grassmarket
Candlemaker Row
Greyfriars
George Heriot's School
Lauriston Place
George Square

High Street
South Bridge
Cowgate
Chambers St
Old College
St Mary's Street
Cowgate
Pleasance

ROYAL MILE

Easter Rd
Regent Road
Leith Walk
Waterloo Place
Calton Hill

Holyrood Road
Dumbiedykes Road

Whitehorse Close
Canongate
Holyrood Abbey
Palace of Holyrood House
Scottish Parliament

Holyrood Park & Arthur's Seat
Salisbury Crags

N
W — E
S

½ km
¼ mile
0

© Helen Stirling Maps 2024. Contains Ordnance Survey Data. © Crown Copyright and Database Right 2024

I

Royal David's City

Nine centuries ago, a scribe sat down at his writing board on a summer's day and with a knife sharpened a quill into a nib. Having dipped it into ink made with oak gall, he began to write history:

> *David dei gratia Rex Scottorum, Roberto electo Sancti Andree et omnibus comitibus et baronibus et omnibus fidelis suis salutem . . .*

David, by the grace of God, King of Scots [to] Robert, Bishop-Elect of St Andrews and to all his courtiers and barons and all his faithful men [sends] greetings . . .

Know that I give and concede in perpetual free gift to the Priory [later the Abbey] of Dunfermline the whole tenth part of all my demesne revenues of Dunfermline, save for those rents which belong to other churches.

> *Et unam mansuram in burgo meo in Strivelin, at aliam in burgo meo de Perth, et aliam in burgo meo de Edenesburg.*

And one toft [house plot] in my town of Stirling, and another in my town of Perth, and another in my town of Edinburgh.

When the scribe at last put down his quill, having been careful with every detail of this legal document, he had indeed written history, the earliest surviving record of the name and existence of the settlement of Edinburgh. The document, known as a charter, was dated 17 July 1124 and was one of a series of grants given by the king. It carried the Great Seal of Scotland impressed in wax and was for the clergy at Dunfermline indisputable proof of ownership of land in three of the king's towns.

As the sixth and youngest son of Malcolm III and his saintly Queen Margaret, David would not have expected to become king. To keep him out of harm's way (for his brothers could be ruthless), his sister, Maud, took the boy south to England where he quickly found himself at the centre of power. Henry I married Maud, and David was styled 'Brother of the Queen' and given land as well as status. As a refugee from the Gaelic-speaking court at Dunfermline and all its roistering martial traditions, David macMalcolm soon became David fitzMalcolm and was raised as a Norman Frenchman. Henry I not only gave him swathes of land in England, he also forced David's brother, Alexander I, to agree to the grant of a vast area of southern Scotland to the young man, the whole of the Tweed Basin and part of Lanarkshire. As Prince of Cumbria, he began immediately to innovate in ways that would have profound influence on the early history of Edinburgh.

Towns were very important to the prince. He owned Berwick, then part of Scotland, and profited greatly from the tax revenues on trade through the busy port. Much of this came from his other large town, one that has completely disappeared. Roxburgh stood at the confluence of the Teviot and the Tweed, opposite Kelso, and it held great markets for the sale of wool and hides that attracted international buyers, merchants from Flanders, Germany and Italy. These goods were exported through busy Berwick. Towns made kings wealthy and powerful.

David's other important initiative showed indirectly how lucrative trade was. In 1113 he brought a community of monks from France first to Selkirk and then to Kelso (to be nearer Roxburgh and its mighty castle) and, just as he did for Dunfermline, endowed them with lavish gifts of land and cash revenues, most of the latter from his towns and their trade. These were freely given for the sake of the immortal souls of himself and his family – piety was profound in the twelfth century as well as transactional – but also because David wanted to modernise, to have his literate, record-keeping monks (who answered directly to him through their abbots) develop the economy and create more wealth.

The toft in Edinburgh that the king gave to Dunfermline is not specifically located, but it was nevertheless a precise term. One of the witnesses to the document, Bishop Robert, commissioned Mainard the Fleming to supervise the layout and building of the new town at St Andrews sometime between 1145 and 1150, and what he did helps visualise how early medieval Edinburgh probably looked. There needed to be a marketplace, and at its eastern end, Market Street in the middle of St Andrews is wide enough to accommodate stalls, which it still does most Saturdays. A toll booth to collect taxes, and houses for tradesmen, merchants and others were also required. For the latter, 'tofts' were pegged out by 'liners'. These plots were usually about 7.6 metres wide and included room at the side for a 'closeur' (perhaps from *closerie*, a French word for an enclosed garden), or a close as it became known, a private passage that allowed access to the backlands, or gardens. In twelfth-century Edinburgh these were probably about 130 to 140 metres long and ran steeply downhill to the north and south.

The enduring shape and subsequent history of the High Street strongly suggest that the liners who laid out King David's town followed Mainard's protocols. Below St Giles' Kirk, the street is more than 30 metres wide, indicating a similar pattern of building to St Andrews. From an early date, a toll booth was built next to the church, in the centre of the new town. The other essential requirement was enclosure and security. Tolls had to be paid by those farmers and producers who wanted to come to the markets, so access was strictly controlled. Stone walls were expensive and out of the question, so ditches were often dug and sowed with 'quickset', impenetrable thorn bushes, and these were almost certainly policed on market days. David's town of Edinburgh was small, limited from the beginning to 143 acres, a restriction that would greatly influence its history for centuries. A church already existed as a focal point. St Giles is very old but was certainly endowed by the king's older brother, Alexander I, in 1120, and the wooden buildings on the tofts of the early High Street stood on either side.

Nine hundred years ago, Edinburgh was not a city, not even a town, but in reality what we might think of today as a village of a few hundred souls where regular markets were held. Unlike St Andrews, Roxburgh or Berwick, it stood on a narrow, steeply sloping site with poor access to natural sources of water. But these awkwardnesses were less important than the reason for Edinburgh's existence – the mighty rock to the west and the fortress that stood on its summit.

2

Fire and Ice

No urban skyline is as distinctive as Edinburgh's. While other cities use notable buildings or structures as visual shorthand, such as the Houses of Parliament, or the Eiffel Tower, Edinburgh has been uniquely blessed by geology. The outline of the Castle Rock with the long tail of the Old Town flowing downhill to the east, and the deep declivities of the Grassmarket/ Cowgate and Princes Street Gardens/Waverley Station on either side, is immediately and universally recognisable. And it is majestic. Anyone looking west from Calton Hill sees a stunning vista, and how geology and history made a city. On one side is the jagged spine of the medieval settlement and on the other the rectilinear formality of the Georgian New Town, while in the centre, leading the eye into the distance, Princes Street runs arrow-straight. Others will argue with passion for their own hometowns but objective observers know that Edinburgh is without rival.

Fire and ice made it so. More than 300 million years ago the crust of the Earth was dangerously dynamic. Volcanic eruptions tore through it, sending vast tonnages of ash and dust rocketing into the atmosphere; rivers of red-and-white hot magma spewed down the flanks of these black mountains; the boom of thunder everywhere rent the air and the ground shook with an elemental violence. Out of such spectacular convulsions Edinburgh was created.

Like the Bass Rock and Traprain Law to the east, the Castle Rock was once the top of a volcanic pipe. Forced from the molten core of the Earth, magma boiled upwards and often found its way out into the air through cylindrical vents. When the eruptions settled, over millions of years, and the magma simmering in the pipes cooled, their tops formed a very hard and rounded shape, known as a volcanic plug. Worn down by erosion caused by the wind, frost and rain of millions of winters, the Bass Rock, Traprain Law and the Castle Rock began to assume their modern appearance.

Some time around 24,000 BC the weather grew unusually severe and stormy in the north, in what was to become Scotland. Temperatures dropped, and snow did not melt in the spring, staying on the hilltops through the summer. The last Ice Age was beginning. Even summer skies darkened, growing seasons shortened, vegetation died back and the animals that depended on it retreated further southwards every year. As the snow fell and the frosts deepened, the early peoples of Scotland also fled, and the landscape emptied and became silent.

At its height the Ice Age created a pitiless white vista, stretching away on every side. It was dominated by the ice domes, huge hemispherical mountains of compacted ice, sometimes several kilometres thick. Scotland was crushed under a massive dome that formed over the ranges north of Loch Lomond. Incessant hurricanes blew around its symmetrical slopes, buffing them smooth, and often the downward flow of wind created sustained periods of anti-cyclone and clear, bright blue skies. It was a landscape of devastating beauty.

The ice obliterated all life, and at its zenith, around 16,000 BC, the glaciers reached down as far as the English Midlands and South Wales. When temperatures at last began to rise, change would be rapid. Within the span of only two or three generations, the ice sheets and the tundra to the south of them would retreat several miles. And as they did so, the impact on the environment was dramatic. When the glaciers on the flanks of the Lomond ice dome groaned and cracked and moved slowly eastwards, they bulldozed our geography into recognisable features. Frozen inside these wide rivers of ice, all sorts of debris were carried along, and huge boulders and pods of gravel scarted and ground across Scotland's midland valley, moving vast volumes of earth and soft stone. When the glaciers at last turned into meltwater torrents, the effect could be almost immediate. River courses were broken out, deep valleys created, and the character of the landscape profoundly altered.

As gravity and rising temperatures drew the Lomond glaciers eastwards, they collided with the hard rock Edinburgh Castle now sits on, and they were forced to divide. Having scoured and buffed the old volcanic pipe down to the bare, sheer cliffs now visible on three flanks, the ice flow scraped out the deep ravines on either side: what became the Grassmarket/Cowgate and Princes Street Gardens and the site of Waverley Station. And crucially for the development and later nature of the city, the glaciers left a long tail in the eastern lee of the Castle Rock, the tail on which David I's medieval town would be built.

It was in Edinburgh that these geological processes were first recognised. In the middle of the nineteenth century, the idea that the northern hemisphere had endured an ice age was still seen as revolutionary, difficult to prove. Some conservative souls still preferred to believe in Noah's Flood as the cataclysm from which God delivered the world. In 1840 the Swiss scientist, Louis Agassiz, arrived in Scotland to tour the Highlands and look for evidence of the impact of glaciers on the landscape. In his native Switzerland, he had noticed that in the valleys below glaciers there were places where rock formations had clearly been smoothed and striated by the movement of ice and the debris locked inside it that had long since retreated. But it was not until he came to Edinburgh that he became certain that Scotland had once been covered by an ice sheet, had been emptied of its people as the land turned white. Agassiz surveyed the western crags of Blackford Hill, to the south of the city, and when he saw the scoring and gouging on the over-hanging rocks and the long tail down to Liberton behind them, he declared 'that is the work of the ice!' His findings marked the beginning of the science of glaciology – and gave *The Scotsman* newspaper one of its greatest scoops.

3

The Pioneers

By 11,000 BC Scotland was at last ice-free. A vast green canopy carpeted the land, trees sprang up over many of the hill ranges, only the wind stunting their growth. Like a temperate jungle, the great wood was dense and often shaded by thick and lush cover as the trees reached up for the light. Willow, aspen, birch, pine and hazel were the first to flourish, and they remain our most hardy and adaptable native trees. Broadleaved oaks, elms and limes followed, and behind them came the animals who thrived in the abundance of the wild-wood. Birds fluttered above the treetops, their songs incessant in the long summers. Squirrels scuttled through the canopy, as did pine martens and polecats. While roe and red deer moved warily among the trees, larger, more aggressive animals – wild boar and the mighty cattle known as aurochs – thrashed through the undergrowth. Aurochs, standing over six feet high at the shoulder and with a horn-spread of seven feet, were giants, as big as rhinoceros. By the streams, rivers and lochs, otters and beaver fished, and waterfowl lived on the rich vegetation.

Predators waited in the shadows of the wildwood. Lynxes, bears and packs of forest wolves stalked the unwary. And behind them came the most dangerous killers of all – human beings. Prehistoric men, women and their families usually preferred to travel by water, and the first pioneers who came north to the Firth of Forth arrived in boats. Probably coasting up from the south, they reached the mouths of rivers and streams first. The outfalls of the rivers around Edinburgh – the Almond, the Water of Leith and the Esk – were almost certainly among the first sites in the Lothians to be colonised. They were good places to live, almost Edenic in a warm summer and a ripening autumn, offering food from the sea, the river and the land – and security. The only tracks through the wildwood were made by animals, and under the dense shade of the crowding trees, it was easy to get lost. Water was always a reliable way to regain a hunter's bearings: follow the fall of the ground to a stream and then follow that until it joins a river, which will eventually find the sea and the familiar shore.

The southern hinterland of the Forth, the place now covered by the centre and suburbs of Edinburgh, was likely the hunting and gathering territory of no more than one extended family, and perhaps one or two satellite groups. But around 10,000 BC it was a workable, familiar environment. Handy landmarks stood high on every side: the Pentland Hills to the south, the unmissable Castle Rock, Arthur's Seat, Blackford and Braid Hills, and Craiglockhart and Corstorphine Hills to the west. It was a defined homeland for the hunter-gatherer-fishers who first came north. And it may well have been a good life. Temperatures had risen close to modern levels, and by 10,000 BC the leaves of a thousand autumns had fallen and enriched the great wood and allowed it to nurture and sustain many animals. A wild harvest of fruits, berries and nuts was available, and the long and well-fed evenings of the late summer on the banks of the Almond or the Esk might well have been pleasant as people took their ease, talked, joked and gossiped. But it proved to be a false arcadia.

Far away to the west a last, devastating legacy of the Ice Age was about to be unleashed. In the north of what is now Canada a vast freshwater lake of ice melt had gathered. Held back only by frozen dams bulldozed into place by massive glaciers, it had begun to leak, at first only slowly. The overspill at first drained south, carving out the great central American river systems of the Missouri and Mississippi. Then, very suddenly, perhaps in thirty-six hours, the mighty lake broke down the ice dams to the east and, with a deafening roar, flooded into the Mackenzie River Basin, out to the Beaufort Sea, the Davis Strait and into the Atlantic Ocean. Sea levels rose by 30 metres overnight and the tsunamis wiped out countless coastal communities, including those on the southern shores of the Forth. Even more disastrously the huge volume of cold freshwater turned the Gulf Stream off course, pushing it away from the coasts of Northern Europe. Almost immediately the weather changed, and the deathly cold crept back over the face of the land. Storms blew, snow lay thick and long, and the pioneers who had survived the tsunamis shivered and fled south.

As the ice dome reformed over Ben Lomond and the western mountains, the north was empty and silent once more. Around the Castle Rock and Arthur's Seat the winds whistled, and although the ice sheets probably did not reach the eastern coasts, the tundra was sterile. For seventy generations, around 1,500 years, it seemed as though Scotland would stay locked in the grip of the ice – but then gradually the weather improved. Out in the Atlantic the clear skies had helped the ocean recover its salinity. The baleful effects of the Canadian dam burst eventually evaporated and the Gulf Stream once again flowed northwards. Snow and ice melted, the trees grew high once again, and very slowly the pioneers returned. The continuous human history of what would become Edinburgh had at last begun.

As the ice melted after what historians and archaeologists have called the Cold Snap, between c. 9400 BC and c. 8000 BC, sea levels rose once more. The Firth of Forth reached as far inland as Aberfoyle, where the bones of whales have been found, and the Clyde also encroached from the west. For several generations the land bridge connecting southern Scotland with the north was only eight miles wide. Much of what became the site of the city of Edinburgh was submerged under the prehistoric sea.

Nevertheless, pioneers did venture north again, and soon after the ice melt. At Cramond gossamer traces of a hunter-gatherer-fisher camp have been found and dated to before 8000 BC. Little more than soil stains now, the site shows where a group, perhaps a family, spent time on what was probably a summer expedition. Perhaps their purpose was to fish and trap animals and preserve their meat by smoking or air-drying. Berries, nuts and fungi could also be dried or roasted to provide good staples through the hungry months of the winter.

With only wisps of evidence to go on, archaeologists have long believed that the early pioneers did little more than rustle the leaves as they moved through the ancient wild-wood. Putting up only makeshift shelters – some of them similar to bender tents, held up and given tension by green stakes driven into the ground and then covered with hides (as seems to have been the case at Cramond) – and lighting fires, theirs was a transient, sparse presence. But a sensational recent discovery near Edinburgh has forced a radical revision of that view.

When routine investigations took place prior to the construction of the Queensferry Crossing, the new road bridge over the Forth, archaeologists uncovered something startling. At Echline in South Queensferry they found the remains of one of Scotland's oldest houses. Dating to c. 8000 BC, it would have resembled a giant tipi. Postholes dug in an oval arrangement held thick tree trunks or boughs and were canted inwards so that they could be secured at the apex. Probably made weathertight with a covering of turf, inside was a shallow pit about seven metres in length and blackened areas where several hearths held fires that burned in the darkness. The house could have happily made a snug home for six to eight people.

If archaeologists find organic matter preserved on a site, they can date it. At Echline they came across hazelnut shells, and since they grow and ripen in only one year, they can give precise results. And this is what turned out to be sensational. It was the shells that showed that the house was built some 10,000 years ago. More than that, its discovery completely dispelled the notion of the pioneers as transients, as shadows flitting through the wildwood. The effort and organisation required to build a solid wooden house more than implies ownership and the exercise of customary rights to the land around; it insists on it. And given the wide area needed to sustain even a small group living in one place (a continuous supply of firewood was only one of the most pressing logistical problems), these customary rights must have been vigorously defended. Their names will never be known, their short lives pieced together only by fragments of archaeology, but it is certain that by c. 8500 BC, the area around Edinburgh had its first recorded inhabitants.

4

The Kings of Edinburgh

Cities and their suburbs obliterate much of the archaeology beneath them. There was almost certainly a house like the great wooden tipi at Echline in the Edinburgh area, but it is highly unlikely that it will ever be found.

No precise date, or indeed the names of any individuals, can be linked to a profound historical event, perhaps the greatest revolution in human history, that took place only a thousand years after the family of hunter-gatherers built their wooden tipi at South Queensferry. In the fertile lands between the rivers Tigris and Euphrates, in much of what is now modern Iraq, animals were being domesticated and wild grasses were being modified and cultivated to produce a reliable annual harvest of cereals. Farming was the greatest revolution in human history, and yet very little is known about how it was developed and adopted. These new ways of producing food reached Scotland around 3500 BC, and the area around Edinburgh was a good place to make them work.

As communities began to create small fields and pastures by clearing the wildwood, sometimes using fire, they looked for places that had natural drainage. Until very recently, as late as the eighteenth century, valley bottoms and flat ground were often boggy and impossible to cultivate. What early farmers wanted was the sort of gently sloping terrain found to the south of the Castle Rock. For example, the ridge now leading from Church

Hill eastwards along Strathearn Road offered inclines on either side steep enough for run-off but not too steep to plough and plant. Terracing was also dug, and the remains of this system can still be clearly seen on the eastern flanks of Arthur's Seat.

Farming pinned people to the particular places they worked on and improved, and, in turn, that commitment fostered ideas of ownership. Competition for fertile land must have taken place, and in the millennia following 3500 BC a hierarchical society developed. In Orkney spectacular farmers' monuments have survived at Maeshowe, the Ring of Brodgar, the Ness of Brodgar and the Stones of Stenness. They suggest a well organised society sufficiently prosperous to afford the time to build these elaborate religious structures – and also a directing mind, either a king or a powerful elite. And the houses at Skara Brae show real sophistication. There is no reason to believe that the farmers of Midlothian were less skilled or successful: the major difference is in the materials they used. They probably built in perishable wood rather than stone, and their sites have seen much more intensive use as waves of historical change washed over the landscape, obliterating almost all traces of the early farms.

One of the most dynamic changes in society was the evolution of the warrior. As family groups coalesced into tribal societies and patriarchs established themselves as chiefs, it is likely that their supporters or bodyguards began to practise specialist military skills. When metal appears in the archaeological record of the third and second millennia BC, it is often found as weapons, not all of them designed for hunting. Swords, for example, were made for one purpose, and that was fighting and killing.

In 1778 Duddingston Loch, at the eastern foot of Arthur's Seat, was being dredged for marl, a carbonate-rich mud used as fertiliser. When the buckets were lifted and emptied onto the banks of the little loch, workmen were amazed to see scores of iron and bronze objects embedded in the mud. Almost all were weapons: swords (including a rapier) and spearheads. Valuable and prestigious objects owned by a warrior elite, they had first been damaged and burned before being thrown into the loch with no intention to retrieve them. It seems they were sacrifices made to the gods whose presence or spirit was associated with water. As they sank to the bottom of the loch, the weapons were preserved in the anaerobic mud for almost 3,000 years. Now the Duddingston Loch Hoard is in the National Museum of Scotland in Edinburgh.

By 1300 BC to 1200 BC it is likely that swordsmen rode horses, what we would call ponies. Terrets, the metal parts of harness, have been excavated, and by the beginning of the first millennium BC, small posses of cavalrymen might have formed the retinues of tribal chiefs, perhaps even of men who could call themselves kings. Hillforts were where they lived, at least for part of the time, and on Arthur's Seat and Easter Craiglockhart Hill stone ramparts and prehistoric ditching have been identified. Most spectacularly, at Newbridge, on the western outskirts of Edinburgh, a chariot burial was discovered. Dating from 400 BC, the chariot had been set into the ground upright and intact. Usually drawn by two ponies yoked to a central pole and driven by one man while another threw javelins or fired arrows, these trim little vehicles were certainly the prerogative of a warrior elite, perhaps even of kings. Burial in a chariot speaks of high status and elaborate ritual, to say nothing of a belief in an afterlife.

The highest status of all probably belonged to the man who ruled from Edinburgh's Castle Rock. Recent archaeology has uncovered evidence of a fortress that was occupied at the beginning of the first millennium BC. Fragments of animal bone, charcoal and other organic material were radiocarbon dated to between 972 BC and 830 BC, and the remains of two roundhouses, the characteristic dwellings of the period, were found. The archaeologists believed that they were part of a larger settlement across the summit of the Castle Rock. No traces of ramparts or defences were discovered, but the dig was very restricted in its scale. These finds mean something surprising – that Edinburgh Castle can claim to have been continuously occupied for 3,000 years, longer than any other site in Britain.

By the end of the first millennium BC it is possible to catch some fleeting sense of what the kings, the warriors and the society that supported them were like. They spoke a Celtic language, but not Gaelic, as might be casually assumed. Place names and later poetry confirm that the rulers of Edinburgh spoke a dialect of Old Welsh. From Caithness to Cornwall this was the common tongue of Celtic Britain. Gaelic was at that time the language of the Irish and, probably, Argyll. The name of Edinburgh itself is partly Old Welsh in origin, although mysterious in derivation.

The modern name has the Anglian 'burgh' attached, a relatively late change, occurring after AD 638 when the Northumbrian armies captured the Castle Rock, calling it 'Etin'. At that time 'burh' meant a defended settlement. The older version of the Edenesburg of the charter of David I was Din Eidyn, and in Old (and modern) Welsh it simply denoted a fortress or a settlement. Eidyn was probably a personal name, perhaps a divine ancestor, perhaps an early king, and it may have stood for the district, the ancient equivalent of Lothian. Which allows a simple but not very informative meaning of the Fortress of Eidyn, whoever he, she or it was.

Much later, Old Welsh poetry composed in the fortress described a warrior society that saw itself in emphatically heroic terms. Glory in battle was the chief end of life for the cavalrymen of Din Eidyn as they spurred their ponies out of its gates and down the slopes of what would become the medieval town.

5

The Emperor and Edinburgh

In AD 79, lookouts on the ramparts of Din Eidyn saw a Roman army marching towards them. Eagle standards glinting and fluttering, flanked by screens of cavalry and led by the governor of Britannia, Gnaeus Julius Agricola, three legions had come to bring the north of Britannia into the empire. And the king on the Castle Rock had agreed to help them do it. Known as the Votadini, later the Gododdin, the native peoples of the Lothians and southern Scotland had probably agreed a deal with Roman emissaries. In return for a decent price for their corn (needed to feed the advancing legions), a degree of independence and a promise of protection from neighbouring kingdoms, the Votadini kings would wave the invasion through their territory.

Agricola chose his line of march carefully, anxious about ambush, and it is likely to have followed Dere Street, the slightly later Roman road which can still be seen crossing Soutra Hill. As it nears Edinburgh, it picks up the line of the modern A7, and then descends to the road junction at Nether Liberton, not far from the Cameron Toll Shopping Centre. Dere Street disappears under houses and modern roads after that point, but historians believe that it may have followed the straight line of Kilgraston Road and Marchmont Road before skirting the western side of the Meadows and crossing the Water of Leith at Dean Bridge. It may have then struck across country to Cramond and the Forth shore.

Excavations on the eastern bank of the Almond have discovered extensive remains of a Roman fort at Cramond (incidentally a near-untouched Old Welsh place name, derived from *Caer Amon*, the 'Fort on the River', the Almond). Built in AD 141, it guarded the eastern flank of the Antonine Wall, a huge defensive earthwork thrown by the legions across the narrow waist of Scotland, between the Forth and the Clyde. The remains of the principia, the headquarters in the centre of Cramond Fort, were found around the modern kirk, and the walls reached down to the Forth shore. Better than any of their enemies, the Romans understood the power of coordinated logistics. While soldiers patrolled the Antonine Wall, sailors and marines watched the shores of the firths at either end. It is likely that the peoples of Fife, which lay outside the empire in 141, were allies of the Votadini and the ships beached at Cramond were ready to cross the Forth to help them in any emergency and to discourage enemy naval activity against them. The ancient name of the Fife tribe, the Venicones, translates from Old Welsh as the 'kindred hounds', and they were likely friendly, corn-producing satellites. The unusual place name of Blebo, near St Andrews, may derive from *Blatobulgium*, which translates as 'the Meal Sack Place', where Roman quartermasters bought grain from native farmers.

To the east of Edinburgh, another Roman fort was established at Inveresk, near Musselburgh. As the attention of emperors was taken up by crises and opportunities elsewhere in their enormous domain, the Antonine Wall and its Forth forts were slighted and abandoned in the mid 160s AD, with the Roman Army retreating to Hadrian's Wall.

Towards the end of the second century AD, rebellion flared once more in the north, the territory that had come to be known as Caledonia, and by 208 the warlike Roman emperor Septimius Severus was mustering a huge army in Britain to deal with it. With more than 45,000 soldiers, cavalry and marines, it was by far the largest ever to invade Scotland. The expedition travelled slowly overland while being shadowed up the North Sea coast by a supporting fleet. As the columns of the Roman vanguard reached the site of their next over-night encampment, the rearguard had only just passed through the gates of the previous one.

When the legions reached the Forth shore, they did some-thing remarkable. Two options presented themselves to Septimius Severus and his commanders. To move further north and into the territory of the native Maeatae, the leading kindred in the Caledonian confederacy who had risen in rebel-lion, they could either board transport ships to cross the Firth of Forth or march west to Stirling and cross the meandering River Forth below the castle rock. They did neither. Instead, the Romans probably built the first bridge across the Forth.

Coins were used to commemorate not only emperors, with their noble profiles on one side, but also great events, achieve-ments and engineering feats on the obverse. A coin minted in 208 showed troops crossing a bridge, and the historian Herodian had heard of plans made by Severus' generals that anticipated water being a barrier to their advance. Another coin shows more precisely how the Romans solved their logis-tical problem.

It shows a pontoon, a bridge of boats. Under it is an exact term – not 'PONS' for a bridge but 'TRAIECTUS' for a crossing, a term found in the English word 'trajectory'. Its probable location suggests a fascinating hypothesis. Historians now believe that this bridge of boats almost certainly crossed the Forth between South and North Queensferry, where the three modern bridges are. The Romans were certainly capable of building a floating bridge across the Forth. At 1,800 yards, it was not the longest pontoon constructed by army engineers

– a much longer one had been thrown across the Bay of
Naples in the reign of Caligula. And geography helped. The
little island of Inchgarvie offered a very useful, midway
anchoring point. The method used was probably very simple:
boats were towed out one by one, lashed together and then
anchored in place with great nets of stones lowered fore and
aft. A roadway was then made across the decks of the boats
and the huge army could march across it on a calm day when
the sea and the tides were placid. The coin shows the Emperor
Septimius Severus crossing it with his son and heir, Caracalla.
The pontoon and another bridge across the Tay at Carpow
were part of an attempt to outflank the army of the Caledonian
confederacy. After the death of Severus in York in 211, such
expensive and ultimately ineffective campaigning ceased, and
the north was left to its native kings for four centuries.

The Votadini ruled from Edinburgh's Castle Rock, but it
was not their only citadel. Traprain Law in East Lothian was
also fortified, and Eildon Hill North in the Tweed Valley, and
Yeavering Bell at the eastern end of the Cheviot ranges. All of
these are singular hills standing relatively clear in the landscape and with wide views around them. High places were
sacred to the early peoples of southern Scotland, but the
choice of the Castle Rock and the other impressive eminences
was also political. No one in the lands around could doubt
where power lay; it was to be found in the glowering forts
where kings sat in judgement, where smoke from their halls
spiralled into the air, and where their warriors gathered. These
were powerful political statements in the landscape.

Votadini is a Roman/Greek version of the Old Welsh name
Gododdin, but its derivation is not very informative, like that
of Edinburgh. It means something like 'the followers of
Fothad', who was perhaps a founding king or a divine ancestor. By the end of the fifth century and the decline and fall of

the Roman Empire in the west, these kings were powerful, in control of the Lothians and the Tweed Basin. They were also becoming Christians, and cemeteries of east/west-facing graves start to appear in the archaeological record. Near the main runway of Edinburgh airport stands an inscribed stone and the remains of around fifty very early Christian burials. The Latin reads: 'In this tomb lies Vetta, daughter of Victricius.' These are probably the first names of people who lived in the Edinburgh area to come to light.

In 600 the Christian kings of the Gododdin faced an army of pagans. Germanic settlers, known as the Angles, had taken over in Northumberland and Yorkshire, and an alliance of native kingdoms had formed to expel them. These warriors knew themselves as Y Bedydd, 'the baptised', and their enemies as 'Y Gynt', 'the gentiles' or 'the heathens'. Led by Yrfai mapGolistan, warlord of Edinburgh, the Gododdin and their allies rode south to Catterick to confront the hosts of the Angles – where they were slaughtered, only a few native soldiers surviving a terrible and savage defeat.

Momentum was with the Anglian kings, and in 603 Aethelfrith routed an army of Gaelic-speaking warriors from Argyll at a place called Degsastan, probably near Addinston Farm at the head of Lauderdale, only twenty miles south of Edinburgh. By 638 the pagans had crossed Soutra in triumph, probably following the relatively intact Roman road, and the Castle Rock fell in that year to the Angles. No more is heard of the Gododdin and their mysterious and ancient line of kings. Their dialect of the Old Welsh language slowly slips into disuse and is now only remembered in place names like Cramond. An early dialect of English becomes the speech of power, the speech of the conqueror, and eventually the language spoken in Edinburgh and all of the early medieval royal towns.

6

English Edinburgh

It was only pressure from the vigorous Pictish kingdoms of the north that prevented the Angles from overrunning all of Lowland Scotland. Decisive defeat at the battle at Nechtansmere, near Forfar, in 685, restricted their territory to the lands south of the Forth, and, in the centuries afterwards, the Gaelic kings of Argyll, eventually the macMalcolm dynasty, gradually pushed them south towards the Tweed Valley, down to where the modern border between England, Angle-land, and Scotland now runs.

At Carham, near Kelso, a pivotal battle was fought in 1018. Malcolm II, King of Scotland, and his Welsh-speaking ally, Owain ap Dyfnawal, King of Strathclyde, inflicted a heavy defeat on the Angles, the people who had become known as the Northumbrians. It secured all of the Lothians and Edinburgh and much of the Tweed Valley. But not before English had virtually completely replaced Old Welsh as the language of the south-east of Scotland and the peoples who lived around Edinburgh.

The Northumbrians left a religious legacy that is still visible in the heart of the city. At the foot of Lothian Road, where it joins Princes Street, stands St Cuthbert's Church, and the dedication offers a hint of its great antiquity. Originating in the Borders, taking holy orders at the monastery at Old Melrose and rising to become Bishop of Lindisfarne, Cuthbert was a talismanic figure for the Northumbrian kings, and it was not long after his death in 687 that he came to be revered as a great saint. *Haliwerfolc* was an early definition of being English: it means 'the holy man's people'. Durham Cathedral is Cuthbert's great monument, but there are many ancient dedications to his exemplary life in the area once ruled by his patrons. Under the relatively modern church of St Cuthbert in Edinburgh (1892–4) traces of six earlier buildings have been found. Dating to the eighth century, the church is probably older than the High Kirk of St Giles (which was only formally a cathedral between 1633 and 1639 when Charles I tried to impose bishops on the Kirk) in the centre of the Old Town. A church dedicated to St Cuthbert was first recorded in the mid ninth century.

The oldest, clearly visible and mostly intact structure in Edinburgh is another church, St Margaret's Chapel. It stands at the highest point inside Edinburgh Castle. Its saint was Queen of Scotland until 1093, the wife of Malcolm III and mother of David I, but the chapel or, more correctly, the small church, was probably commissioned by her son twenty or so years after her death.

In 1128 King David founded another church, one that would change the destiny of Edinburgh. He gave Holyrood Abbey a site at the foot of what is now the Royal Mile, a good place to build a church, as well as the flat ground around it that has become the Queen's Park. David was inspired by his sainted mother and her ownership of a precious relic known as the Black Rood of Scotland. Allegedly a fragment of the True Cross (the Rood), it gave its name to the new foundation of Holyrood and immediately brought pilgrims who wished to be close to the cross on which Christ had been crucified. Its monks were canons regular and eventually they were allowed to found their own town, the Canongate.

Around the abbey was a wide area of sanctuary where debtors and those accused of crimes could shelter from pursuit by the law. They appealed to the Bailie of Holyroodhouse and, if granted sanctuary, were given lodgings and could not be arrested. The tenements on either side of the Abbey Strand may be descendants of where these people lived. Metal 'S' letters on the Royal Mile and elsewhere remember the boundaries of the sanctuary.

From the early fourteenth century Scottish kings were holding regular parliaments in the abbey church (usually the only buildings large enough to accommodate all those who attended were the major churches) and lodging in the 'King's Chamber'. Accommodation expanded, and James II was born at Holyrood in 1430 before being crowned in the abbey six years later. James IV had a royal palace built between 1501 and 1505. More than the castle, which may have been draughty as the winter winds whistled around the rock, the foundation of Holyrood did a great deal to establish Edinburgh as royal capital – replacing Dunfermline and other centres like Stirling – and make it, eventually, Scotland's capital city. The present palace of Holyroodhouse is largely the result of later remodelling, much of which was completed by the end of the seventeenth century.

Further uphill, David I's town was laid out around the old church of St Giles. What is now the Castle Esplanade was originally much too narrow for housing, and in any case the garrison would have been happy to have a clear, uncluttered field of fire from the eastern ramparts. It is said that the gatehouse is a bowshot from the first building on Castlehill. It was only in 1753 that the narrow ridge was broadened into a parade ground using the earth from the foundations of what is now the City Chambers. The Esplanade was widened again in 1816 and railings added.

Castlehill, the westernmost element of the Royal Mile, recalls the narrow ridge and was probably not an important part of the medieval town. Where the street broadens dramatically is at the Lawnmarket. Derived from Land-market (an echo of the longer vowels of early Scots pronunciation –'lawnd' was how 'land' sounded), the place where farmers brought produce from the landward area to sell, the street was also laid out to accommodate stalls and booths. It narrowed significantly at St Giles, the place where the Old Tolbooth intruded and made the High Street only twelve to fourteen feet in width. This ramshackle building was the centre of civic and commercial life in medieval Edinburgh and even later. Finally demolished between 1811 and 1813, it was where tolls were paid by merchants and stallholders, where the nightly curfew bell was rung and where town meetings and law courts were held. Eventually it became a jail and a place of execution. The site of the Tolbooth is marked by a heart-shaped design picked out in coloured cobbles, near St Giles. It is also a reference to Sir Walter Scott's novel, *The Heart of Midlothian*, which is set in the Old Town of Edinburgh and features the Tolbooth as a location. Local people sometimes surprise passing visitors by turning and spitting on the design, often without pausing. They do it for luck, and it is said that when prisoners were at last released from the filthy cells of the old prison, the first thing they did was to spit in a gesture of defiance.

Beyond the Tolbooth the High Street widened again before reaching its end at the east gate, the Netherbow Port. The layout of medieval Edinburgh's spinal street resembled an egg timer, and off this pinched waist, at one time, around 200 closes and pends ran downhill on either side.

As the town grew, some of the closes evolved into specialist markets that traded most days. Fleshmarket Close and

Fishmarket Close are the most obvious, and the grain and meal markets were held nearby, behind St Giles. Around the Tolbooth and the old kirk, luckenbooths huddled. Simply meaning locked stalls, they usually sold more valuable items. Most of the luckenbooths were set up in a narrow alleyway between the Tolbooth and St Giles. Many were located between the buttresses in what was known as 'Stinkand Style', a name that needs no explanation. Merchants with street frontages on the Lawnmarket and High Street were encouraged to build arcades over the entrances to their shops as Edinburgh's importance as a market town steadily grew in the later Middle Ages. By 1260 the Merchant Company of Edinburgh was founded to protect the trading rights of its members, and as trade with the Baltic increased, the Masters and Mariners of Leith were granted a royal charter in 1380. It allowed them to levy a tax on imports known as the prime gilt. Money was beginning to jingle in the pouches of the traders and tradesmen of Edinburgh.

7

The High Life

The precipitous fall of the ground of Edinburgh's High Street, the restricted area of 143 acres and the increasingly crowded nature of the site began to force expansion upwards. By 1400 it was the largest town in Scotland, with more than 350 buildings loosely described as houses and a population of about 2,000 souls. By 1500 the High Street was continuously built up and the Grassmarket and the Cowgate had become part of the town. Pressure on space forced the tenements to add more and more storeys. Buildings with six or seven floors were not uncommon, and visitors to Edinburgh were awestruck at their height. By the seventeenth century the Great Tenement, which stood near what is now the Signet Library, had climbed to a dizzying and dangerous fourteen floors.

In *Guy Mannering*, his novel of 1815, set in the 1760s, Sir Walter Scott used his own experience of the Old Town, just as the vertiginous tenements were about to pass into history:

It was long since Mannering had been in the street of a crowded metropolis, which, with its noise and clamour, its sounds of trade, of revelry, and of licence, its variety of lights, and the eternally changing bustle of its hundred groupes, offers, by night especially, a spectacle, which, though composed of the most vulgar materials when they are separately considered, has, when they are combined, a striking and powerful effect upon the imagination. The extraordinary height of the houses was marked by lights, which, glimmering irregularly along their front, ascended so high among the attics, that they seemed at length to twinkle in the middle sky. This coup d'oeil, which still subsists in a certain degree, was then more striking, owing to the uninterrupted range of buildings on each side . . . formed a superb and uniform Place, extending from the front of the Luckenbooths to the head of the Canongate, and corresponding in breadth and length to the uncommon height of the buildings on either side.

The difficulties of Edinburgh's site were obvious and not helped by the exigencies of politics. To protect Edinburgh from a feared siege in 1460, James II had a dam built at the east end of the site of Princes Street Gardens. Fed by springs at the foot of the Castle Rock, the Nor Loch filled up. Dark and filthy, it clearly prevented expansion in that direction. Elsewhere the growing landed wealth of the Church had a similar blocking effect.

In the east, Holyrood Abbey and the Augustinian canons had established their own town, the Canongate. To the south the convents of Blackfriars and Greyfriars (Dominicans and Franciscans) held land they were not willing to give up. In 1513, in the panic that followed the king's death in the catastrophic defeat at the Battle of Flodden, a wall incorporating earlier fortifications was hurriedly thrown around Edinburgh. This effectively stifled any expansion beyond it. The Flodden Wall survives in places, at the Pleasance and south of the Grassmarket, and it shows how small the medieval city was.

The high buildings off the High Street, the Grassmarket, and their closes and pends, were known as tenements. All manner of people, poor and wealthy, titled and anonymous, could share a common stair, and the survival of many tenements, rebuilt over centuries, has maintained a defining tradition. Several thousand people still live and work in the centre of Edinburgh, and something of the domestic, human scale of the Old Town (and the New Town) as well as a sense of community still survives. Unlike other great cities, it does not see all of those who work there leave for the suburbs to be replaced by those coming into town to eat, drink and make merry. In the period of Victorian expansion, architects imitated the style of the medieval tenements and created areas of dense settlement immediately to the south of the Old Town. The long rows of two-up and two-down terracing so typical of English cities is not seen in Edinburgh until the outlying suburbs, mostly built in the twentieth century.

When in 1143 David I allowed the abbey to set up its own town, the Canongate, it remained separate from Edinburgh until 1643, and its last vestiges of independence were not abolished until 1856. Because it was adjacent to the royal residence, noblemen built houses in the Canongate, and these aristocratic associations survive in the shape of Queensberry House, Moray House, Panmure House and Acheson House. The little town was not walled, though it was enclosed by large ditches, and its original open, less built-up character can still be glimpsed. The Canongate Tolbooth fared better than Edinburgh's and still stands, while several closes remember the town's role as a staging post for coaches and their horses. Preferring to avoid the steep climb up the High Street at the end of a journey, travellers and their transport lodged at the White Horse Inn, at White Horse Close, and in the other old hostelries which still line the main street.

The king also gifted the right to build and make money from mills on the Water of Leith to the Augustinian canons at Holyrood, and the district of Canonmills was the busiest location. And Holyrood Park, particularly the area nearest the Canongate known as the Queen's Park, was a handy place to graze animals and gather fuel. David I gave a wide tract of wild and wooded land to Edinburgh for the same purposes. The Burgh Muir lay to the south of the Burgh Loch (later drained to become The Meadows) and it reached the foot of Blackford Hill. From east to west it stretched for three miles from Duddingston to Morningside. Now it is almost entirely overlaid with the suburbs of south Edinburgh, but in the twelfth-century documents relating to Holyrood Abbey it was a 'great forest full of harts and hinds, foxes and suchlike manner of beasts'. David I and his descendants were enthusiastic huntsmen, and around their properties the chase was often possible. Buildings began to go up on the Burgh Muir in the late sixteenth century, mainly the houses of local lairds, and now its only remnant is Bruntsfield Links. It is still common land, and even though it is home to an ancient golf course, the people of Edinburgh have the right to use it.

Scottish kings bestowed other, more generous gifts. Because the Stewarts gradually adopted Holyrood as a royal residence, power and power-seekers gravitated to Edinburgh in their wake. At the outset of the fifteenth century the Scottish Parliament, the Three Estates, was in the habit of being peripatetic, like the royal court, but by 1500 it had more or less settled in the city, convening in the castle and at Holyrood Abbey. When James V decreed in 1532 that the Court of Session and the College of Justice should also sit in Edinburgh, it had become de facto the capital place of Scotland. The city can date its pre-eminence from that time.

The continued royal preference for Holyrood meant that the castle had to find other, more everyday functions. A cannon foundry was fired up and barracks built. In 1573 the eastern defences were badly damaged by an English army sent to intimidate Mary, Queen of Scots and her supporters. David II had built an elaborate tower between 1368 and 1377 that guarded the main entrance to the castle and looked down over the town below. It also contained private royal apartments. But when English artillery cast down its walls, they were not replaced. Instead, the Half Moon Battery, curved better to withstand a barrage, was raised up on the foundations of David II's tower on the orders of the Regent Morton, and a portcullis gate added.

As Edinburgh Castle diminished as a political focus, power began to attach itself to the burgesses who lived in the growing town down the hill. In 1482 James III had granted them a greater measure of autonomy. A town council had evolved, and both merchants and craftsmen formed themselves into associations. But James III's Golden Charter allowed the Edinburgh provost and bailies to dispense justice, acting like county sheriffs. These men grew very influential, and the city's government stayed in their hands until the Burgh Reform Act of 1833.

The jurisdiction of the town council was unambiguous. The Flodden Wall of 1513 marked its extent, and in the early sixteenth century it was kept in good repair. From the Netherbow Port at the foot of the High Street it ran south down St Mary's Street (the house frontages themselves had formed part of the original makeshift defences) and from there climbed up the incline of the Pleasance before turning right and west along the ridge of Lauriston Place. It then turned north to reach the bottom of the Castle Rock at the West Port. There three roads met, and on the arch of the old gate the heads of traitors were traditionally spiked. The burgesses maintained the Flodden Wall less out of a concern for defence (occasionally it was little more than someone's back garden wall) and more as a means of defining the city. Municipal income derived mainly from customs paid on goods coming in to Edinburgh's markets, and while the Flodden Wall would not have resisted an army, or even a regiment, it did deter smugglers.

In the sixteenth century the economy boomed. As the city settled into its role as a capital, commerce followed. Between 1501 and 1597 the revenue collected on goods multiplied from £1,758 to £8,833. And the population rocketed, doubling from 12,500 in 1516 to more than 25,000 a century later, making it one of the most densely packed urban populations in Europe. The smoke from countless unswept chimneys, concentrated in a small area, gave rise to the nickname Auld Reekie.

In his epic poem, *Marmion*, set at the time of the Battle of Flodden, Sir Walter Scott saw the city from afar. The sentiments sound more like the author's than those of Lord Marmion, the fictional hero, when he first catches sight of Edinburgh:

> Still on the spot Lord Marmion stay'd,
> For fairer scene he ne'er surveyed.
> When sated with the martial show
> That peopled all the plain below,
> The wandering eye could o'er it go,
>
> And mark the distant city glow
> With gloomy splendour red;
> For on the smoke-wreaths, huge and slow,
> That round her sable turrets flow,
> The morning beams were shed,

And tinged them with a lustre proud,
Like that which streaks a thunder-cloud.
Such dusky grandeur clothed the height,
Where the huge Castle holds its state,
And all the steep slope down,

Whose ridgy back heaves to the sky,
Piled deep and massy, close and high,
Mine own romantic town!

Much of the romance of Edinburgh swirled around its history, and Scott was the acknowledged master and inventor of the historical novel, often creating fictional characters as actors in real events. His feel for the twists and turns of history that unfolded in its streets was unrivalled.

8

Commerce in the Cowgate

In the sixteenth century Scotland was one of the least urbanised countries in Europe. Only 3.5 per cent of its people lived in towns with a population of more than 2,500. Almost every Scot worked on the land or was in some way associated with food production. For mercantile transactions, cash mattered, but food, especially in the shape of rents in kind, was a much more important and common currency for ordinary people, and a barter economy dominated, no doubt with exchange rates fluctuating in times of glut or shortage.

Such towns as there were all looked much like Edinburgh with a central, often single, street with closes and wynds (the latter were public thoroughfares, while closes, as the term implies, were private and sometimes gated) running off it. It is still possible to see that arrangement in Edinburgh's High Street, despite modern distractions, with its herringbone pattern, a spine with rows of parallel bones on either side. But perhaps one of the best-preserved royal towns is Lauder in the Scottish Borders. Flanked mostly by two-storey houses, the high street widens in a funnel shape stop-ended by the medieval toll booth and two further streets on either side wide enough to accommodate stalls and carts with farmers selling produce off the back of them.

By 1500 Edinburgh's population had grown to 10,000, making it by some distance the largest town in Scotland, if not quite yet a city. At that time, Glasgow had a population of about 2,500. Smaller towns like Lauder ran markets that served the local economy, but through a regrettable accident of history, Edinburgh had become internationally significant. After the Wars of Independence had ravaged the farms, villages and towns of the Tweed Basin, and severely and repeatedly disrupted the local economy, Edinburgh began to grow quickly in importance. As English armies continued to raid, firing and plundering fertile Berwickshire and Roxburghshire, output collapsed in the fourteenth and fifteenth centuries. With its three churches, great castle, grammar school and royal mint, the town of Roxburgh began to shrivel and then eventually disappeared. But most vital was the occupation and eventual loss of Berwick to the English. It had been David I's most successful royal town, its customs revenue for a time exceeding London's as its trade, and the associated tolls became a very lucrative source of income for the exchequer. Companies of Flemish and German merchants were based in Berwick, but when it fell into English hands, the town lost its agricultural hinterland and therefore its raison d'être as a port and a market. Scottish Border farmers were discouraged from paying customs dues to the officials of an English king, and instead they went north with their produce, to Edinburgh.

After being occupied for much of the fourteenth and fifteenth centuries, Berwick was finally lost to England in 1482. In 1500, the Edinburgh burgesses were complaining that they were too busy because of the 'greitt confluence of simpill peipill' – the common people rather than important producers and merchants who came to the fourteen markets in the town. In south-eastern Scotland, there was nowhere for them to go if they wanted to sell produce, especially for export. Through its port of Leith, Edinburgh had become by far the busiest exporter in Scotland. And what the town exported was mostly animal products.

Especially in the autumn, after a summer on lush grass to fatten them, a huge number of animals were herded along the Cowgate to be slaughtered. In one year, 1499, Edinburgh processed and exported 44,325 sheepskins, 28,740 skins of other animals (mostly goats) and 24,347 cow hides. In all, 97,412 animals were stunned with a poleaxe before having their throats cut so that the blood (for black and other puddings) could be collected by butchers. The noise of terrified animals must have been deafening as they fell to their knees and died. Butcher meat was sold daily in Fleshmarket Close and elsewhere but most of it was salted in barrels for export through Leith. From the pans at Prestonpans and elsewhere on the Forth shores, great quantities of sea salt were produced.

The skins of the slaughtered animals were perhaps the most valuable commodity and the process of converting them into leather was also eye-watering. The tanning of hides in the Cowgate, especially towards the Grassmarket end, was a labour-intensive and very smelly business. After the horns and hooves had been cut off (and they had their uses), the skins were scraped before being immersed in pits filled with dog droppings or lime, and then sprinkled with urine to help remove the hair. The hides became leather when they had been immersed in tannin, an astringent got from tree bark.

This 'odiferous' trade drove out people who could afford to move from the south side of the town, and eventually the tanners themselves were forced to move. Tanfield, in the north of the city, well beyond the old walls, remembers their exile.

The stench was not much missed, unlike another odour that used to be characteristic of the Cowgate until very recently. Women enjoyed certain rights and privileges in royal towns. The wives and widows of burgesses, the wealthier merchants who controlled the government of Edinburgh, ran the brewing trade. In 1530 there were 288 female brewers making beer in the town, and the savoury-sweet smell of their product no doubt permeated the air. Until the end of the twentieth century, the biscuit scent of brewing (and the implied promise of a pint of heavy) floated over the city's rooftops, and nowhere more so than in the Cowgate. Scottish & Newcastle made beer at its foot but eventually had to make way for the Scottish Parliament, built on the site of the brewery in the late 1990s.

9

Edinburgh Reformed

By the middle of the sixteenth century what was perhaps the most turbulent and incendiary phase of Edinburgh's long story was about to crackle into life. For decades Europe had been convulsed by the conflicts dividing the church, what became known as the Reformation. By 1560 Scotland had ceased to be a Catholic nation, at least in name, and one of the most energetic and famous reforming ministers was John Knox. What may well have been his house still stands in the High Street, and it is a superb example of Edinburgh's late medieval style of architecture. Described as a sermon in stone, there is a sculpture of Moses (also serving as a sundial) on one corner and an inscription, 'Love God Above All and Your Neighbour as Yourself'.

The reforming mob omitted to take this advice seriously as they set upon the properties of the church around Edinburgh. The Franciscan friary on the site of Greyfriars Kirk was burned down in 1558, and the Dominican convent of the Blackfriars was pillaged and destroyed a year later. Its location is remembered by Blackfriars Street. Here is what a contemporary diarist remembered:

Upon the 14th day of July . . . the Black and Greyfriars of Edinburgh were demolished and cast down utterly, and all the colleges and chapels about the said burgh with their yards [outbuildings] were likewise destroyed, and the images and altars of St Giles Kirk destroyed and burned.

Perhaps the most regrettable casualty of all that zeal was the church of the White Friars, the Augustinian canons at Holyrood. But reforming fury was not entirely responsible for its ruination. In the time of the Rough Wooing, when Henry VIII of England was attempting to effect a dynastic marriage by force, his armies burned the beautiful church in 1544 and three years later stripped the lead off its roof. Holyrood Abbey was as near as Edinburgh came to a cathedral in size, but perhaps for that reason the mob had no love for the old building, and in 1570 much of it was pulled down.

Near a roundabout that links the Grassmarket and Candlemaker Row with the Cowgate there stands a little-noticed cradle of Scotland's history. In 1560 the Magdalen Chapel was the unlikely centre of a revolution. It housed the first General Assembly of the Church of Scotland. The Scottish Parliament had abolished Catholicism, made the Mass service illegal and established the Reformed Church as the national church. As the ministers of the new establishment, many of them former priests, packed into the Magdalen Chapel, the voice of John Knox was heard. He was one of the founders of modern Scotland and, far from being a dour, hectoring killjoy, he did much that was positive to shape contemporary society.

In the chapel, the General Assembly appointed a commission headed by John Knox to write the new church's constitution, and by a quirk of fate his colleagues in this great endeavour were John Winram, John Row, John Spottiswoode, John Willock and John Douglas. Between them, the Six Johns compiled what was known as the First Book of Discipline. Its guiding principle was to reverse the direction of church govern-ance. Instead of a top-down administration such as the Vatican, who appointed bishops and told them what to do and the bish-ops controlled priests and their parishes, the congregations of Scotland were given the right to elect their ministers. This change was of enormous importance since the minister was a vital individual in every town, city and village. And it was a very different approach from the Church of England, where vicars were appointed by bishops, often on the recommenda-tion of the gentry and the aristocracy.

Education was seen as crucial to the reformed church in Scotland, which became known as the Kirk. Martin Luther and Jean Calvin had vigorously promoted the doctrine of the priesthood of all believers. This could hardly be more differ-ent from the Catholic Church, where the Mass was conducted in Latin and priests were the intermediaries who alone spoke to God. Instead, reformers believed that each individual ought to be responsible for their own salvation. That in turn required everyone to be able to read the Bible for themselves – which of course required literacy.

In other writings, John Knox insisted that every parish was to have a school and a schoolmaster to 'teach grammar and the Latin tongue'. He went on: 'Further, we think it expedi-ent that in every notable town there be erected a college, in which the arts, at least logic and rhetoric, together with the tongues [languages], be read by sufficient masters for whom honest stipends must be appointed.'

The immediate difficulty for the Kirk in this great, civilis-ing enterprise was that it had no money. As the property of the great churches and abbeys was broken up, much of it was seized by the nobility and the crown. Consequently, it took centuries for Knox's dreams to be completely realised. After the feverish activity in the Magdalen Chapel, literacy became near universal but only by the later eighteenth and early nineteenth centuries. This was Knox's great achievement – and the enduring legacy of the Reformation and the Book of Discipline that was written in the Cowgate.

10

The Town's College

Edinburgh benefitted particularly, and immediately, from the reformers' insistence that education would light the path to salvation. The oldest school in the city, the Royal High, was probably founded by the canons at Holyrood. After the wreckage of the mid sixteenth century, it moved to the garden of the ruined Dominican monastery at the foot of Blackfriars Street, and the traditional colours of its pupils' uniforms might be an echo of the black-and-white habits worn by the brothers. Remembered in the street name of the High School Yards, the Royal High flourished on its new site, and it was vigorously and famously independent. When a town bailie came to the school to sort out a dispute over holidays, one of the boys shot him dead at the gates.

As a result of the particular nature of the Scottish Reformation, education became a defining and creative force in Edinburgh's development. Known originally and simply as the Town's College, Edinburgh University grew up near the site of the Royal High School. But not after a substantial delay and a row. In 1557 Bishop Robert Reid left 8,000 merks, a substantial sum, in his will to build a college in Edinburgh. An influential diplomat, he had been educated at the University of St Andrews between 1511 and 1515. As Edinburgh grew in importance, Reid believed it needed an institution that could offer further education. There were already three other universities in Scotland at Glasgow, Aberdeen and St Andrews, while England rubbed along with only two (and by 1600 there would be five Scottish universities with two in Aberdeen in the shape of King's College and Marischal College). Reid left enough money to provide for teachers of grammar (meaning Latin and possibly Greek grammar), the arts and law, with all the necessary accommodation for students. The turmoil of the Reformation delayed the implementation of Bishop Reid's bequest, and when the burgesses attempted to extract the 8,000 merks in the late 1570s, his descendants refused to cough up. Eventually King James VI brokered a compromise, and the founding charter was sealed in 1582.

All of Scotland's other universities had been founded by papal bulls and were very ecclesiastical in nature, focusing at first on divinity and training literate priests. Edinburgh was the first to be created by a secular authority, and it was immediately known as the Tounis College. It is the oldest non-ecclesiastical university in Britain and was an immediate success. Between eighty and ninety scholars enrolled, and classes were run by Robert Rollock, a graduate of St Andrews. It seems that he was the sole teacher and was expected to instruct and examine all subsequent intakes. In 1587, the first forty-seven students to graduate (or be 'laureated') were given the degree of Master of Arts, a particular designation in Scotland that has persisted.

At first making use of the buildings around the ruined Kirk o' Field, the university eventually moved into what is now called Old College in South Bridge. Surely one of the most beautifully proportioned buildings in the city, it was designed by Robert Adam, who died before its completion, and concluded in 1827 by William Playfair. On the Old College dome stands the Golden Boy, a gilded youth carrying the torch of learning.

For much of the early history of the university, there was continuing tension in its relationship with the town council. The latter had a great deal of control, overseeing staff appointments and deciding which subjects were taught and examined. In 1704 the council seized the university's records and refused to cooperate unless certain demands were conceded. Nevertheless, it expanded, founding faculties of law and arts in the early eighteenth century. Edinburgh became the first in Britain to teach English Literature, and the Faculty of Medicine began its distinguished history in 1726, eventually becoming pre-eminent in the world. By the end of the eighteenth century, the reputation of the university was at its zenith: Voltaire called it 'a hotbed of genius', Benjamin Franklin believed that the teaching staff were 'a set of truly great men, Professors of Several Branches of Knowledge, as have ever appeared in any age or country', and the third president of the United States, Thomas Jefferson, believed that its teaching and research in the sciences was unmatched, remarking that 'no place in the world can pretend to a competition with Edinburgh'. He advised his son-in-law to study at the university.

Despite its accumulating prestige, relations between the Tounis College and the town did not improve. What started as a harmless snowball fight in the quadrangle of Old College in January 1838 got out of hand. It developed into a two-day battle between students and the local residents of South Bridge. After failing to persuade the rioters to desist and disperse, the lord provost was forced to call on the garrison of Edinburgh Castle. It was only when faced with ranks of soldiers with fixed bayonets and the threat of a fusillade that the students backed down, although a few snowballs were thrown. Relations have, it is said, improved between town and gown since then.

11

The Rider with the Ring

At Richmond Palace near London, on 24 March 1603, an old lady was dying and an age was passing. Queen Elizabeth I was approaching seventy, very old for the times, and she appeared to have fallen into a deep depression after the recent deaths of several close friends. Staring in silence out of the windows of her chamber for hours on end, she looked unsteady at times, and her ladies-in-waiting arranged cushions on the floor around her. When the old queen at last sank down, her chief minister, Robert Cecil, told her she must go to bed. At that moment the famous Tudor temper flared for perhaps the last time: 'Must is not a word to be used to princes, little man!'

Childless and unmarried, Elizabeth had never explicitly named an heir, but it was widely expected that her closest living relative would succeed to the throne of England. James VI of Scotland was her cousin, both of them descendants of Margaret Tudor, wife of James IV, Queen of Scotland and the daughter of Henry VII. But nothing was certain. James had been in regular contact with Robert Cecil and through him had sent assurances to all of his colleagues on the privy council that their positions would be secure after the queen's death. The Scots king was nervous. Other candidates waited in the wings. A Catholic conspiracy could emerge. European kings might intervene. And so he hatched a plan. Once Elizabeth died, speed would be essential, or so he thought.

Sir Robert Carey had been an English March Warden, a professional soldier charged to keep the reivers on both sides of the border in check, a man who knew his way around in all senses, and someone who was also very ambitious and well-connected. His sister, Philadelphia, Lady Scrope, was one of the old queen's ladies-in-waiting and she became closely and crucially involved in what happened. King James had written often to Elizabeth I, his tone following the advice of Robert Cecil, and he had also sent gifts. One was a ring with a blue stone, almost certainly a sapphire, and the queen was so pleased that she had said she wore it always. When she died at about 3 a.m. on Thursday 24 March, Philadelphia pulled the ring off Elizabeth's finger and opened a widow in the upper chamber. In the courtyard below, her brother was waiting, his horse saddled. And Philadelphia threw the ring down to him.

There then began a remarkable journey. Changing horses at pre-arranged stops, Robert Carey rode like the wind for Edinburgh. By early afternoon on Saturday 26 March, no doubt exhausted, he reached the fords over the River Tweed at Norham. Somewhere on the Scottish side, his horse spooked and threw him. While Carey lay on the ground, it kicked him in the face, its shoe gashing him badly. Having pressed on, in some pain and badly bruised, through East Lothian, Carey at last clattered into the cobbled courtyard of Holyrood Palace and banged on the great oak doors. His cloak and boots caked in mud, cut and bloodied down one side of his face, the messenger from London roared that the king should be woken immediately. Servants scattered, but finally Carey was admitted to the royal bedchamber. He knelt and was the first to acknowledge James VI of Scotland as King of England and Ireland, and as proof that it was so, he gave him the old queen's ring. From that moment on, the history of Edinburgh moved in a new and different direction.

A week later, the King of Great Britain and Ireland went to St Giles. After the sermon, he stood up to make a speech, saying goodbye to the people of Edinburgh in their parish church and promising to come back every three years. In fact, he did not come back north until 1617, and that did not go well.

When at last the king departed, having had to borrow money to fund his cavalcade, he rode eastwards to Musselburgh on the old north road. Less than an hour after his departure from the Palace of Holyroodhouse, a touching incident took place, one that showed James VI and I in a rather better light, and one that also reminded him of the fragility of power. He was forced to stop and dismount in Musselburgh, where his party met the funeral cortege of Robert Seton, the Earl of Winton. He had been one of the party who rescued his mother, Mary, Queen of Scots, from Loch Leven Castle and had been a lifelong supporter of the Stewart dynasty. Out of respect, King James moved aside, took off his hat and sat on a dyke in silence as the mourners passed.

A day later, a cannonade boomed out over the Tweed estuary from Berwick Castle as the king was welcomed into his new realm. At York he was given the keys of the city and, in an ironic twist, lavishly entertained at a house in Buckinghamshire as a guest of Sir Oliver Cromwell, the uncle of the man who would later sanction James' son's execution. What might have been a frantic dash southwards had turned into a relaxing royal progress as it became clear that the succession was uncontested. After taking a month over a journey that Robert Carey had completed in less than three days, the new king came to the grand house of Robert Cecil, the second most important man in England. There he was feted by the English nobility, who bowed and gave their fealty as they led his horse through the grounds and courtyards of the mansion. It was at that moment, rather than in the later ceremonial entry into London, that the accession of James was confirmed.

By the end of April 1603 Edinburgh no longer played host to a royal court. And, as important, the noblemen and their families who lived in the Canongate and in the city were also leaving for the south. Preferment required propinquity, and they hoped for continued favour at Westminster, not thinking twice about abandoning Holyrood. In any case there might be rich pickings as the old regime was replaced by the new in a much wealthier and more prosperous country. History had moved on. James VI and I and his dynasty had left Edinburgh behind, and the town looked elsewhere for its destiny.

12

Jinglin' Geordie, Mary, Watson and Stewart

Edinburgh turned away to other concerns, and to a growing – and particular – interest in education. Following in James VI's train, in April 1603, was a colourful character whose wealth and decency changed the face of what was now becoming a city and no longer a town. George Heriot's purse jingled with many coins, for he had made a considerable fortune as a goldsmith and moneylender, and James VI and his queen, Anne of Denmark, had been favoured clients. It seems highly likely that he helped finance the royal cavalcade that eventually reached London, and when the court settled there, so did Jinglin' Geordie.

Queen Anne was said to love jewellery of all kinds, and Master Heriot supplied much of it on credit. In 1609 she owed him £18,000 plus interest, and between 1605 and 1615 he made for her necklaces, earrings, lockets, a gold case with her initials picked out in small diamonds on the lid, and many other pieces. They were all valued at the staggering sum of £40,000. Jinglin' Geordie made a great deal of money, but it seems that what he wanted most of all had eluded him. When he died in 1624, he had no legitimate children, although he made bequests to two natural daughters as well as nieces and nephews. Jinglin' Geordie's huge fortune was to be spent on the maintenance, relief, upbringing and education of poor, fatherless bairns, the sons of the freemen of Edinburgh. George Heriot's Hospital, now the school which stands in Lauriston Place, was the result, and its opening in 1659 began a long and honourable tradition in Edinburgh.

There were thirty pupils in the school's first year, all of them orphans, and since then, Heriot's has maintained the founder's wishes, continuing to provide free education to a large number of children who are being raised by widows, or widowers, although more students did pay fees as time went on. In the quadrangle, there is a statue of Jinglin' Geordie, and the Latin motto under it translates as: 'This statue shows my body, this building shows my soul.'

Such moving sentiments were clearly related to the legacy of the Reformation, the Book of Discipline and John Knox's aspiration to see mass literacy in Christ's Kingdom of Scotland. A priesthood of all believers could only come into existence if they could be taught to read the Word of God for themselves. And that priesthood included all immortal souls, those of women as well as men.

In 1694 the Merchant Maiden Hospital opened. The school was the result of the generosity of Mary Erskine, a remarkable woman who made her fortune by setting up a private bank. Like George Heriot, Mary was childless, having lost her three boys and two girls in infancy. Her endowment had a very specific purpose: it was for the maintenance (and education) of the daughters of burgesses in the city of Edinburgh. The Merchant Maiden Hospital was first in the Cowgate (the tanning pits having moved north by that time), but Mary later gave more money to buy a house and garden beyond the walls at Bristo, not far from Heriot's. It was a pioneering enterprise, one of the very earliest girls' schools in the world.

More enlightened philanthropy followed in 1704 when
Mary Erskine founded the Trades Maiden Hospital to provide
education for the daughters and granddaughters of 'decayed'
(meaning either old, unfit or unemployed, or all three) craftsmen. It was opened in what is now West College Street, just
off Chambers Street. These institutions flourished, but the
vision of their extraordinarily far-sighted founder was never
forgotten. In 1944 the Merchant Maiden Hospital was
renamed The Mary Erskine School.

Much impressed by the Merchant Maiden Hospital, the
Trades Maiden Hospital and the school founded by George
Heriot, George Watson made bequests to them all in his will
in 1723 but left the residue of his fortune to found a new
school. What became George Watson's College was for 'entertaining and educating the male children and grandchildren of
decayed merchants in Edinburgh'. Before moving to its present
site in Colinton Road, the college was on the north side of
George Square. Watson was the first chief accountant of the
Bank of Scotland when it was founded in Edinburgh in 1695.
Unusually the conditions of his legacy extended beyond
schooling. The governors were to be responsible for former
pupils until they were twenty-five and pay them an allowance
as they took up apprenticeships (these were not paid jobs in
the eighteenth century; sometimes apprentices paid their
masters for the privilege) or the early stages of professional
careers. However laudable all of this philanthropy was, it had
some darker origins. It is almost certain that part of Watson's
great wealth came from investments in a ship that was engaged
in the slave trade.

When Daniel Stewart died in 1814, he left a sum of money
to be invested. When it reached £40,000, it was to be spent
on the foundation of a school for needy boys in Edinburgh.
It was built on the site of the present Daniel Stewart's School

in Queensferry Road. Stewart's College became Stewart's Melville when it merged with Melville College (founded in 1832) in 1972, and they were later twinned with Mary Erskine's.

When the first boys came to Heriot's, they wore a 'sad russet' uniform and black hats. The idea was that all the scholars would look the same and no distinction would be made between the better-off and those less so. Edinburgh's streets still see thousands of schoolchildren on weekdays in their distinctive uniforms: maroon for George Watson's, navy blazers trimmed with scarlet at Stewart's Melville, navy blazers and tartan skirts for Mary Erskine's, and blue and grey for Heriot's. To some, the fee-paying schools of Edinburgh smack of privilege, and that is true, but they are also a living testament to a long history, a particular, cultural devotion to the importance of education.

Daniel Stewart, George Watson and the other philanthropists could have left their fortunes to their families or any number of other causes. The traditions they helped found are still robustly alive, sustained by former pupils' associations and the likes of their famous rugby clubs. Heriot's FP, Watsonians and Stewart's Melville FP used to be closed, accessible only to those who had attended the schools, but their excellent facilities are now open to any who wish to play.

When the 1872 Education Act provided for free schooling for all children, Edinburgh saw the establishment of a series of new schools. Amongst the earliest was Broughton High School in 1887 and, later, Boroughmuir High School on the south side of the city. Like the Merchant Company schools, they formed former pupil rugby clubs that fostered a sense of community in particular areas of the city, their clubhouses and facilities a focus. Boroughmuir Bears is now one of Scotland's most successful clubs.

Edinburgh education is famous across the world for other reasons than antiquity. In Muriel Spark's novel *The Prime of Miss Jean Brodie* the eponymous heroine – who taught what she considered to be '*la crème de la crème*' at the Marcia Blaine School for Girls – embodied a set of paradoxical attitudes. While she always championed the supreme value of education, for girls as well as boys, Miss Brodie was also an admirer of 1930s European fascism and was especially fond of Mussolini. The Marcia Blaine School was apparently based on James Gillespie's in Marchmont, where Spark had been a pupil.

The second great fictional educational creation to come out of Marchmont was again based on a real and eccentric school for girls. A motto of Light and Joy and a liberal curriculum (with no homework) were the hallmarks of St Trinnean's. When the artist Ronald Searle encountered some of the girls during the Second World War, he drew a picture of genteel chaos. The St Trinian's films became legendary, and the portrayal of the headmistress by Alastair Sim was a beautifully observed caricature of certain Edinburgh middle-class attitudes. Having been brought up in the city, he knew them well.

Another famous literary character of modern times was educated in Edinburgh. Ian Fleming's James Bond was expelled from Eton but accepted as a pupil by Fettes College. It was a handy biographical detail that might have explained (but didn't really) the fact that when Mr Bond first appeared on film, he happened to have a strong Edinburgh accent. In reality, Sean Connery went to Tollcross Primary School, though he did make it through the hallowed portals of Fettes at a young age, not as a pupil but as a milkman – one of the many jobs he had at the beginning of his road to stardom.

13

Not Roman Law

Like his grandson, but without a wealthy new kingdom, James V was always on the lookout for new ways to raise cash. Scotland's parish churches, friaries, monasteries and nunneries all paid an annual tax directly to the pope in Rome. It was known as Peter's Pence, and with the help of Bishop Robert Reid, the founder of Edinburgh University, James V petitioned the Medici pope Clement VII for a part of it. There was, of course, a price, one that bequeathed something enduringly distinctive to Scotland, and it was based in Edinburgh.

In October 1517 Martin Luther nailed his ninety-five theses to the door of All Saints' Church in Wittenberg and set in train events that would lead to the great convulsion of the Reformation. Pope Clement wanted to keep Scotland in the Catholic community, and his strategy was to create as many institutional links as possible with those nations as yet relatively unaffected by the teachings of Luther and others. In exchange for a piece of Peter's Pence, James V agreed to reshape Scots law to bring it into conformity with canon law, the legal precepts that governed the Catholic Church.

The College of Justice was brought into being. Based in Edinburgh and organised on a Roman model, complete with senators and other paraphernalia, it was funded by 10,000 golden ducats paid by Scottish bishoprics and monasteries. There were fourteen full-time judges, half of them temporal lords and half ecclesiastics, all governed by a lord president. Bishop Robert Reid was one of the first senators. This institution turned out to be dynamic and effective, and not only did it survive the Reformation, despite its papal origins, it ensured that Scots law began to become distinct from English law. And also that it would be based in Edinburgh, making the city the legal, as well as the political, capital of Scotland. But Scots law was not, as some believe, based on the laws of the Roman Empire but on canon law, dispensed from Rome.

The Court of Session was established by an act of the Scottish Parliament in 1532 and quickly set up. It remains the supreme civil court of Scotland. It began with both clerical and lay judges who were appointed by the king's privy council, and the chief minister, the lord chancellor, presided. There are now thirty-five senators or judges who also sit in the supreme criminal court, the High Court of Justiciary, known simply as the High Court. By 1640 membership of the College of Justice was restricted to laymen only. Crucially, the Treaty of Union of 1707, when the Scottish Parliament ceased to exist and its members went to Westminster, explicitly noted that the Court of Session was to retain its powers and its distinctiveness 'in all time coming'.

While masons worked on the building of George Heriot's Hospital in the first half of the seventeenth century, Edinburgh's town council worried about the loss of the royal court. Money as well as status had leaked out of the city, and anxious that they might lose the Scottish Parliament and the Court of Session as well, they set about providing better accommodation. Both bodies had been forced to use the dingy Old Tolbooth, and neither were happy. On the site of the manse of the minister of St Giles, Parliament House was raised, and it contained the stunning Parliament Hall and new courts of justice. The hall is covered by a remarkable hammerbeam roof and lit by a dazzling stained-glass window in the south gable end. It commemorates the institution of the Court of Session below a stunning portrait of an enthroned James V, bathed in an ethereal light. As Gavin Dunbar, Archbishop of Glasgow, complete with mitre and crosier, gesticulates, a red-robed lay judge looks at him, raising his arm as though making a point of order while another judge reads a document. It looks as though the Court of Session began as it meant to go on, with an argument. Lawyers still pace up and down in this stately space, under the hammerbeam roof of Parliament Hall, whispering to their clients before and after appearances in the adjacent courts.

The Faculty of Advocates (not barristers) and the Writers to the Signet (solicitors) are both associated with the College of Justice and have the right to appear before its judges. Barristers from England and Wales do not have a right of audience and in recent years have been denied, despite at least two attempts.

The Advocates Library in Parliament Square, next to St Giles' Cathedral, was founded in 1682, and the magnificent Signet Library above it was completed in 1822. Both are adornments to the city, and one is now visited by more than lawyers. Known as the Colonnades at the Signet Library, it is now advertised as a high-end venue for 'Edinburgh's finest afternoon tea', where light fare and fizz are served in a genteel, historic salon lined with fluted Corinthian columns.

14

Jenny and the Dean

What is often mistakenly known as the English Civil War also deeply involved Scotland and Ireland, and some of the sparks that ignited the conflict that is more correctly known as the War of the Three Kingdoms first flew in Edinburgh. When Charles I tried to impose bishops on the Presbyterian Church of Scotland (and briefly make St Giles a cathedral), he met outraged opposition. Since the early reforming measures of the 1560s and 1570s, Scottish divines had been developing a radical and extraordinary doctrine. They came to believe that Scotland was a nation specially covenanted to God. In Christ's Kingdom of Scotland, Andrew Melville, Principal of Glasgow University, had taken by the sleeve Charles' father, James VI, and informed him that he was 'not a head, nor a king but merely a member', and in any case 'only God's silly vassal'. The Scots were a chosen people, chosen by God.

Charles I had to be persuaded to come to Edinburgh in 1633 to be crowned King of Scotland. Why couldn't it be done in London? Delays went on for years. When the Scots insisted, Charles decided to make a political statement. He came north with a vast retinue of more than 3,000, including a detachment of 350 fully armed soldiers, 150 English noblemen and his entire royal household. Two hundred carts pulled by a thousand horses brought this deliberately extravagant cavalcade into Edinburgh. The last thing Charles looked like was a Scottish king.

Scone Abbey had been destroyed by a mob of reformers, incited by John Knox, and so it was decided that the coronation should be held in Holyrood Abbey, in the Chapel Royal. It too had been damaged, but expensive repairs were carried out as the royal cavalcade made its way north.

On 18 June, as an overwhelmingly Presbyterian crowd lined the Royal Mile, a calculated, colourful and clearly expensive ritual began. Out of the castle gates, the royal procession emerged and made its stately way downhill to Holyrood Abbey. Portraits of Charles I by the great Flemish painter Anthony van Dyck were hung along its route, and wine flowed freely for the watching crowd. In front of the king in his coach, bishops dressed in gorgeously decorated copes with jewelled croziers and mitres walked past a crowd more used to ministers in clerical grey and black berettas. When the bishops entered the Chapel Royal, there was a great deal of kneeling before the altar. It must have seemed to many that the king was planning a return to what amounted in their eyes to Catholicism. The day before, the chapel had seen a Catholic Mass celebrated by Charles' French queen, Henrietta Maria, and Charles was crowned in Edinburgh according to the Anglican rite. At best, Charles appeared to be promoting the unification of the Church of Scotland with the Church of England.

Two years later, appearances became reality. Archbishop William Laud's Book of Common Prayer was to be introduced to Scotland – to Christ's Kingdom of Scotland – and it provoked a famous and incendiary reaction, the first in a chain of events. On Sunday 23 July 1637, at St Giles, a stool flew through the air. It was thrown at the head of James Hannay, Dean of Edinburgh, as he began to read from the

Book of Common Prayer. The new liturgy had been largely the work of Laud, even though he had no formal authority in Scotland and even though no Church of Scotland minister had been consulted in its compilation. The high Anglican tone in a deeply Presbyterian nation sparked immediate trouble.

Jenny Geddes was a street stallholder with a Sunday sideline as a 'waiting woman', someone who would arrive early at a service to claim and keep a place near the front of the congregation for whoever was willing to pay. As she stood up and hurled her stool at Hannay, she roared at him, 'De'il gie ye colic, the wame of ye, fause thief; daur ye say Mass in my lug!' No translation needed. The stool started a riot, the congregation walked out, the Edinburgh mob was marshalled and the first steps were taken down a path that would lead to war between the king and many of the people of his three kingdoms.

The walkout and the riot were in fact not spontaneous. Two years before Dean Hannay ducked, it had been announced that the Book of Common Prayer would be introduced in Scotland. But events in Edinburgh's High Street almost ran out of control. When Bishop David Lindsay tried to quieten the congregation – it was the women who were most vocal – he was shouted down as 'the spawn of the Devil' and 'a pest on God's kirk', and bibles were thrown at him. The lord provost had to summon his constables, and they cleared St Giles. But the women continued to hammer on the doors and chuck stones at the windows.

A mob had gathered outside on the cobbles. The Bishop of Edinburgh was jostled but managed to get into his carriage despite a hail of stones that spooked the horses. The lord provost was attacked and stoned, and it was only his constables firing over the heads of the crowd that prevented more serious injury. He and his bailies were besieged in the Tolbooth. Remarkably, the lord advocate, the king's chief legal officer (it seems, in name only) began to negotiate with the mob's leaders. In what smacks of prior agreement, he suggested that they, the rioters, set up a committee to negotiate with the privy council. Riots broke out all over Scotland as Laud's liturgy was read from pulpits, and by December of 1637 the lord advocate's committee, known as the Five Tables, had in effect become the government of Scotland. A coup d'état had taken place in Edinburgh.

The Chosen People

Edinburgh had never witnessed an event on the scale of what happened at the end of February 1638. It may be that as many as 60,000 people converged on the city to sign the National Covenant. It was revolutionary, a popular uprising. The terms of the covenant made Charles I's kingship conditional on his maintenance of Presbyterianism in Scotland. If he did not fulfil this duty, then he could be legitimately removed. All innovations such as the introduction of bishops were rejected, and to sign the covenant was not rebellion but a simple acknowledgement that Jesus Christ was the head of the Church in Scotland. And not the king. That meant Charles could not impose anything or attempt to control the Kirk. The architects of the National Covenant were the Reverend Alexander Henderson and Archibald Johnston of Warriston, a lawyer who would later become a senator of the College of Justice. He left a diary entry that recounted the events of that fateful day:

Upon Wednesday 28th February, that glorious marriage day of the Kingdom with God . . . I met all the gentlemen [the nobility] going up the street to the Kirk [of Greyfriars]. I resolved to read and did read the parchment itself publicly which, after some few doubts of some, was approved. And after a divine prayer from Mr Henderson most fit for the time and present purpose, the Covenant was signed first by the noblemen and barons all that night until 8. [By] Thursday morning I had written in the night four principal copies in parchment. At 9 [a.m.] it was signed by all the ministry: at 2 by the burghs [burgesses].

The Earl of Sutherland was first to step up. Within days, most of the population of Edinburgh had come to the kirkyard to add their signatures, evidence that a degree of literacy had been achieved, to say nothing of the spread of political and religious radicalism. After the extraordinary events at Greyfriars, copies of the National Covenant were sent all over Scotland and widely supported except in the Highlands and the north-east. Like the Israelites of the Old Testament, the Scots were now a covenanted people for there now existed a bond between them and their God.

Behind the locked doors of Glasgow Cathedral, in December 1638, the first General Assembly of the Church of Scotland for twenty years was brought to order. In the presence of the king's commissioner, the ministers, elders, lairds and burgesses made sweeping changes. Henceforth, there were to be no bishops in the Kirk. Bishop Robert Lindsay of Edinburgh and all the others were deposed and excommunicated. All was done in the name of 'Christ's Crown and Covenant' on behalf of the 'godly commonwealth of Scotland' and no consideration whatsoever was given to the king's wishes. But many in the cathedral must have been fearful, for the two sides were on a collision course, and who would defend the godly commonwealth?

The Thirty Years' War was raging in central Europe as Catholic states fought those whose rulers had converted to the Protestant cause. Copies of the National Covenant had been sent abroad so that those Scots who were fighting as mercenaries (most of them in the armies of the Swedish king,

Gustavus Adolphus) could have the opportunity to sign. One of the war's most able and experienced generals, Alexander Leslie, organised a muster for his regiment in Germany so that the men could add their signatures. News of events in Scotland accompanied the covenant, and Leslie immediately brokered an agreement with his Swedish commanders. In late 1638, at the same time as momentous events were unfolding in Glasgow, ships carrying companies of battle-hardened, well-equipped Scottish soldiers docked at Leith, and Leslie led them into Edinburgh. Suddenly the National Covenant became much more than pious words. Christ's Kingdom of Scotland had an army.

In part because they would not be easily persuaded to vote him the necessary cash to raise an army of his own, Charles I could not risk summoning a parliament at Westminster. Their mood might have inclined them towards the sort of political opposition that was boiling in Scotland, and in any case the king had not called a parliament for eleven years. Instead, his generals were forced to muster a poorly armed militia at York and then march north. They were 20,000, and Alexander Leslie had 12,000, but they were of a very different calibre, companies of passionately Presbyterian volunteers stiffened by Leslie's mercenary officers and sergeants.

When the Covenanter army marched out of Edinburgh and fortified the singular hill of Duns Law, the royalists had reached Berwick, about fifteen miles away. As a mercenary soldier whose priority was to keep his men alive, Leslie did something that surprised the pious ministers who accompanied his army. He sent word to royalist officers that he would be pleased to entertain them at dinner in Duns Castle. Once the last glass of claret had been drained, the general invited his guests to inspect his well-organised and well-armed troops and the fortifications on Duns Law. The commanders of the king's forces wisely concluded that they should return to Berwick and seek a negotiated peace.

Archibald Johnston of Warriston led the delegation of Covenanters and agreed a ceasefire, and also made some concessions. The radical decisions made in Glasgow Cathedral should be set aside and a session of the Scottish Parliament should convene in Edinburgh in a year's time.

As Warriston may have known, or judged, the 1640 parliament turned out to be even more radical. Probably meeting in the dingy old Tolbooth on the High Street, it voted to replace the Five Tables with a Committee of Estates controlled by the nobility, the lesser lairds and the burgesses of the royal burghs, but with no place for ministers. Parliament denied that the king had the right to prorogue it, and with the Triennial Act, it agreed to meet every three years whether the king summoned it or not. It also assumed the right to vet membership of the privy council and the College of Justice. These revolutionary precepts were soon adopted by the Westminster Parliament, and Britain, and Scotland, began to take sides as war seemed inevitable.

At the end of August 1640, Alexander Leslie led his army out of Edinburgh to fight their first engagement at Newcastle, and as history moved south, these experienced Scottish soldiers played a key role in the first phases of the War of the Three Kingdoms.

The epochal events that took place in Greyfriars Kirkyard may seem like a nation asserting itself, like the early stirrings of a version of democracy in their refusal to accept the rule of a despotic, inept and ultimately misguided king. But these admirable sentiments were not by any means the whole story. The Reformation in Scotland, the National Covenant and the creation of the godly commonwealth had a very much darker side, and horrific scenes took place on Castlehill, the High Street of Edinburgh, in the Tolbooth and at Holyrood Palace.

16

The Burning City

In 1608, in Edinburgh, a group of eight convicted witches were tied to stakes with ropes to be burned alive. In front of a huge crowd, several tar barrels, shovelfuls of coals, wooden kindling and even peat were piled up around the screaming women and set alight. As the flames and sparks leaped high in the wind, onlookers gasped and probably jeered at the appalling suffering taking place in front of them as sackcloth shifts and hair caught fire. But the blaze burned through the rope bonds of three of the women and, blackened and scorched by dreadful burns, they broke free and stumbled out of the raging, crackling pyre – only to be caught by the baying crowd and thrown back in.

These horrific scenes took place at the top of Castlehill, where it meets the open ground of the Esplanade. And they were not uncommon. Scholars believe that 300 women and a few men were burned at what became known as the Witches' Well. A plaque and a modern trough on the wall of the old Castlehill reservoir marks the place where more people died dreadful deaths than anywhere else in Scotland. This period of extraordinary cruelty, of mass hysteria, was not unique to Scotland. In the later sixteenth and seventeenth centuries, witch-burning took place all over Europe. But north of the border, it was an obsession. On either side of 1600 around 500 witches were murdered by various methods in England, but in Scotland, a country a tenth of the size, more than 1,500 were tried, tortured and burned. Part of the reason was legal. In Scotland, the Kirk had insisted it was a crime to be a witch, whereas in England it was an act of witchcraft that was criminal, and that could be harder to prove.

James VI was obsessed with witchcraft and wrote a book about it in 1597. *Daemonologie* takes the form of a philosophical dialogue between two characters, Philomathes and Epistemon, and it begins:

> The feaefull aboundinge at this time in this countrie, of these detestable slaves of the Devil, the Witches or enchanters, hath moved me (beloved reader) to dispatch in post, this following treatise of mine . . . to resolve the doubting . . . both that such assaults of Satan are most certainly practised, and that the instruments thereof merits most severely to be punished.

This amounted to royal approval of what happened at the top of Castlehill, but it was by no means the sole source of encouragement. Christ's Kingdom of Scotland was a godly commonwealth that could not be polluted and could 'not suffer a witch to live', and communities sought to identify and punish witches with a deadly enthusiasm. And nowhere more so than in Edinburgh and the Lothians, where almost a third of all witches in Scotland died.

James VI took an active part. When he returned from Denmark with his prospective bride, Princess Anne, his ship was assailed by a storm. Witches were blamed, and in particular a coven that was said to meet in the Auld Kirkyard in North Berwick was implicated. One of these unfortunate women, Agnes Sampson, was questioned by the king at Holyrood Palace and tortured in order to extract a confession. Deprived of sleep by her jailers, she was pinned to the wall of her cell by a witch's bridle, an iron device forced into her mouth that pressed sharp barbs on her tongue and into her cheeks. After enduring two days of agony, she of course confessed and was burned at the stake. Most witches were either strangled or drowned before their limp bodies were tied to the stake, but others, like the women of 1608, were burned alive ('worryit' in Scots). It was seen as a necessary process of complete extirpation, the removal of Satan's servants from the godly commonwealth.

17

Tipple Town

Before he walked out onto the scaffold set up in London's Whitehall on 30 January 1649, King Charles I, for once, remembered his Scottish heritage. To fortify himself, for he was anxious that the cold might make him shiver and appear to be trembling in fear of what was about to happen, he drank a glass of claret. In the historian Billy Kay's memorable phrase, Edinburgh, Leith and much of Scotland was at that time 'knee deep in claret'.

The origins of this national love of the red wine from Bordeaux are old, stretching back to 1295 when Scotland and France came together in the Auld Alliance, an enduring treaty between the two countries that sometimes made England feel surrounded. With cargoes of Scottish hides, woolfells, cured fish and other staples, ships sailed out from Leith and down to the Gironde estuary, where they were given the privilege of first pick of the new vintages. In the sixteenth century, an aggrieved English merchant complained about this special relationship the Scots had: 'Because he [the Scot] has always been a useful confederate to France against England, he has [the] right of pre-emption or first choice of wines in Bordeaux. He is also permitted to carry his ordnance to the very walls of the town.'

When English merchants arrived at the mouth of the Gironde, they were stopped, had to surrender their arms, apply and pay for passports and were subject to curfew.

In 1560 the Scottish Reformation threatened to sever links with largely Catholic France, but it happened that many of the people of the Bordeaux region were also attracted to the ideas of Luther and Calvin and became Huguenots. In any case, Scotland had developed a distinct thirst for claret, but it was not the dark red, richly flavoured drink it is now. Claret is an anglicisation of the French word *clairet*, and it described a dark rose that suited Scottish tastes in another way. It was cheaper – and therefore widely popular. In the early eighteenth century, Edinburgh poet Allan Ramsay sang its praises:

> Guid claret best keeps out the cauld
> an drives awa the winter soon
> It maks a man baith gash an bauld
> an heaves his saul ayont the mune

which translates as:

> Good claret best keeps out the cold
> and drives away the winter soon
> It makes a man both wise and bold
> and sends his soul beyond the moon.

Barrels of Bordeaux claret were landed at Leith's Wine Quay (the location is uncertain, probably lost beneath the modern port) and taken to merchants' cellars. The sole survivor of these is The Vaults in Giles Street, now the headquarters of the Scotch Malt Whisky Society. Scottish rates of duty on wine imports were historically low, but despite that, vast quantities of claret were smuggled into the country in what was known as 'the fair trade'. St Anthony's Hospital in Leith benefitted greatly because the canons were entitled to a quart (two pints) from every cask that was landed on the Wine Quay. No doubt much of this was settled in cash by the merchants, but perhaps on a draughty winter's night the clergy enjoyed a quart or two. All that remains of the hospital's possessions is a ruined chapel on the flanks of Arthur's Seat.

Barrels needed bottles, and from an early date the production of glass began in Leith. Off Salamander Street – so named because it was widely believed that these cold-blooded, lizard-like reptiles could survive in fire – a major glassworks was established in the mid eighteenth century, replacing an earlier seventeenth-century works behind Sandport Street. At its height in the nineteenth century, there were four huge furnace cones turning out enormous numbers of bottles including the eponymous 'Leith Bottle'. The glassworks also played an important part in the Enlightenment, supplying scientific vessels to Edinburgh University.

The site was convenient because glass manufacture needs a lot of sand and seaweed, and both were close at hand. There is some evidence that Leith saw the development of the modern shape of wine bottles. In the past these had looked like a mason's wooden mel (mallet), rounded, with a flat bottom and a slim neck. But as the quality of the wine improved and needed to age, bottles that could lie on their sides and breathe through their corks were required: the cylindrical shape we see now. The glassworks at Salamander Street punctuated the Leith skyline until 1912 when they were demolished. A housing development was recently proposed for the forgotten site, and before construction began, archaeologists found several old bottles. Sadly, they were all empty.

Nathaniel Johnston & Fils, wine merchants based in the Bordeaux region, are 'negociants', the descendants of emigrants from Scotland in the late seventeenth century. Successful and much respected, they are a memory of the Auld Alliance and a time when claret flowed into Leith.

18

Gala Days in the High Street

Edinburgh's High Street was the stage for all sorts of grisly spectacles, and some were orchestrated to achieve the maximum effect and exposure. Long before newspapers or other media that could broadcast news, justice had to be seen to be done, and seen to be done by as many people as possible. Executions were often occasions for holidays so that the crowd might be as large as possible. The derivation of a 'gala' day is uncertain but it might come from a 'gallows' day. One of the most memorable, best-documented gallows days took place in 1650.

For a year, from the summer of 1644 until September 1645, James Graham, the Marquis of Montrose, and the MacDonald general, Alasdair MacColla, had fought a spectacular campaign in Scotland in support of King Charles I. But after defeat at Philiphaugh near Selkirk, Montrose had fled. In 1650, Montrose returned to raise a Highland army for Charles II but was defeated in the north and then betrayed. From that moment on, his fate was inevitable.

Mounted, humiliatingly, on a carthorse, Montrose reached Edinburgh with his captors on a cold Saturday afternoon in May. Handed over to the city's hangman, he was tied to a seat in a cart, facing backwards, and trundled up the High Street through strangely silent crowds. Criminals bound for execution were usually pelted with rubbish and worse, but here was a dashing soldier who had won astonishing victories against the odds, and it seems that on that spring afternoon, Montrose commanded respect. After a night in a cell in the Tolbooth, he was arraigned in front of the Scottish Parliament where the appalling death sentence for a traitor was handed down.

On the following morning, Montrose dressed in his finest clothes: a scarlet coat over a white linen sark with a lace collar, silk stockings, white gloves, ribboned shoes and a broad-brimmed hat. Before he set that on his head, Montrose carefully combed out his long dark brown hair. He was by all accounts a handsome man, and one of those who watched his preparations thought he looked as though he was going to a wedding rather than to his death. When one of the Presbyterian ministers sent to try to extract some sort of confession complained that he was paying too much attention to his appearance, Montrose is said to have replied: 'My head is still my own. Tonight, when it will be yours, treat it as you please.'

By the early afternoon, a huge crowd of many thousands had gathered in the High Street, and as Montrose was led out from the Tolbooth on his last journey, they did not call out, spit at him, bay or jeer. Instead, there was a low, rumbling, atavistic murmur of anticipation. A grisly spectacle was about to take place. By the Mercat Cross, east of St Giles, where the High Street opened out and more people could see, a high gallows had been erected on a wooden platform. Once soldiers had pushed back the crowd and forced a path, Montrose climbed up its steps with his masked executioners. He had been refused permission for any last words, a gallows speech, and, instead, the hangman carried out his instructions. To further humiliate the marquis, he hung around his neck on a piece of string a laudatory account of Montrose's campaigns. How are the mighty fallen was the none too subtle message.

As was the custom, the condemned man handed over a few

coins to his executioner, payment for a speedy, efficient death. Leaning against the stout beams of the gallows was a wide ladder. After he had tied Montrose's hand behind his back, the hangman guided him up the ladder and slung the noose around his neck before pulling the knot tight. There was a pause, the marquis shouted, 'God have mercy on this afflicted land!' and then the hangman pushed him off into eternity.

At that moment, as Montrose's body swung, the crowd will have gasped. If his neck did not snap, his face will have turned blue as he choked, his body convulsing, instinctively kicking his legs, looking for footing in the air, urine darkening his scarlet breeches. So that as many as possible could see that a brutal justice had been done, Montrose was left hanging from the gallows for three hours. And to prolong the effect even longer, the hangman then hacked off his head and set it on a spike on the Tolbooth where it rotted for eleven years.

In 1660, when the Stuarts were restored to the throne, the gallows were erected and the crowds gathered once more in the High Street. Montrose's skull was removed and replaced on the Tolbooth by the freshly decapitated head of his great adversary, Archibald Campbell, Earl of Argyll.

19

Tee Town

St Andrews constantly claims to be the home of golf. It is not. The rules of the modern game were first compiled in Edinburgh, the first international match was played there, the earliest instructions on how to play the game were written down in Edinburgh, the first members of the royal family to play golf did so in Edinburgh, and the very earliest mention of the game was made in the city. St Andrews is not the home of golf; Edinburgh is, or, more precisely, Leith is.

Games involving hitting a small ball with a long stick were apparently played in medieval Holland, but no serious student of the game believes that golf was not invented in Scotland, in Edinburgh, at Leith Links. Few Dutch golfers have made much of a mark. However, it is true that the name of the game does seem to derive from *colf* or *colve*, the Dutch word for a stick. Perhaps it does. Nevertheless, the game was first noted in Edinburgh and with disapproval. When the Scottish Parliament met in the Tolbooth, it passed an act in 1457 forbidding the playing of 'the gowf' (and football) because it was interfering with the necessary business of archery practice. There was more disapproval to come. Mary, Queen of Scots was the earliest recorded female player and she played gowf in the spring of 1567 in Edinburgh after the murder of her husband, Lord Darnley. When his house at Kirk o' Field was blown up and his body found nearby, it was

thought that the young queen should have been in mourn-
ing, indoors in her widow's weeds, reading the Bible. But
instead Mary was whacking a ball around what was known as
the 'links-land'. These were coastal areas of sandy soil that
could not be cultivated and where beasts were often pastured
on the tough marram grasses. Sheep scrapes, places where the
animals made sandy indentations to shelter from the sea
winds, became hazards for golfers and got the name of
'bunker' from the Scots word *bunkart*, an earthen bank that
could be used as a seat. 'Links' is from *hlinc*, an Old English
term that meant 'ridges' or 'rising ground', a reference to the
sand dunes and the undulating grassland behind them.

The earliest courses noted in the historical record are to be
found in and around Edinburgh. Bruntsfield Links, on the
rising ground south-west of The Meadows, is mentioned
specifically as a golf course in the seventeenth century, long,
long before anything at St Andrews. It is some distance from
the sea, but the soil is sandy and the ground undulating. Golf
is still played there, mostly in the summer evenings, and it is
free and open to anyone. Rather than the three, four and five
hundred-yard holes of most courses, it is a pitch and putt
course, and players need only a short iron or a wedge and a
putter. This is almost certainly how golf used to be played.
Rather than long, par five holes that need tremendous power,
the version played on Bruntsfield Links is about accuracy and
skill: three is a good score, two even better.

The featherie balls used by early golfers were so expensive
that players were careful not to lose them, and their value
gave rise to some of golf's characteristic nomenclature.
Caddie was the name given to porters and also men who
guided those who paid them to their homes in Edinburgh's
dark and dangerous nighttime streets and closes after a
night's carousing, and it was adapted by those golfers who

wanted someone to carry their clubs. But a second caddie was also employed to stand in the fairway at what seemed like a reasonable distance a player might hit the ball off the tee. This man was a 'fore-caddie', and if the precious featherie ball was heading for a long tangle of rough ground, an anxious player would shout 'fore!' to alert his caddie to keep a close eye on where it landed.

The earliest recorded coaching advice came from a Bruntsfield player in 1697. Thomas Kincaid liked to play in the evening after his supper and his approach was thus:

I find that the only way of playing at the Golf is to stand as you do at fencing with the small sword, bending your legs a little and holding the muscles of your legs and back and arms exceeding bent or fixed or stiff and not all slackening them in the time when you are bringing down the stroke (which you readily do).

Not much has changed.

Leith Links was a five-hole course that extended across what is now Salamander Street to the shore before it was cut off by the building of the railway in the middle of the nineteenth century. Usually played twice, to make a round of ten holes, the course was used by what is generally accepted to be the oldest golf club in the world. It eventually gave itself the sonorous title of the Honourable Company of Edinburgh Golfers. The oldest surviving set of rules was codified at Leith in 1744, and whatever the Royal and Ancient Golf Club may claim, all subsequent versions have been based on it. In essence, the Leith rules formed the basis of the modern game. The Honourable Company moved from the links to Musselburgh, which is the oldest course still to be played – not the Old Course at St Andrews – and from there they migrated to

Muirfield in Gullane, where the Open Championship is occasionally played.

In 1744 the club trophy at Leith, a silver golf club, was won by an Edinburgh surgeon, John Rattray. A year later he enlisted in Prince Charles' rebel army and, after the disastrous defeat at Culloden in 1746, found himself in Inverness Jail. His sentence of death by hanging, for he had committed treason, was later commuted after an impassioned plea from Duncan Forbes of Culloden, a steadfast government supporter and the lord president of the Court of Session. He was also a fellow golfer. After his release in 1747, John Rattray resumed his membership at Leith Links and won the silver club on two occasions, his political beliefs not a handicap.

20

Banks in the Wars

The late seventeenth century saw the beginnings of another tradition in the city. In 1695 the Bank of Scotland was founded, a year after the Bank of England. A year later, it became the first in Europe to print its own notes. The present headquarters is on the northern flank of the Old Town, built on a platform near the top of The Mound. It dominates the cityscape, like a classical temple to money. In the beginning the new bank enjoyed monopoly powers, granted by the Scottish Parliament, but after the catastrophic failure of the Darien Scheme (Scotland's attempt at colonialism in Central America) and the Act of Union with England in 1707, these were removed, and in 1727 the Royal Bank of Scotland was brought into being and based in Edinburgh.

The rivalry was more than commercial. The Bank of Scotland lost its monopoly chiefly because it had been involved in raising cash to support the 1715 Jacobite Rebellion. Its political sympathies were Tory, and the Whig government of the time needed a counterbalance. The Hanoverian and Whig-supporting Royal Bank of Scotland supplied it, and for a generation the two institutions were ferocious rivals in what were known as the Bank Wars.

It was the Royal Bank that went on the offensive with a brutally simple strategy. Both rivals issued banknotes that 'promised to pay the bearer' essentially in coin if a note was

presented. In those early years this was not a theoretical trans-
action. And so the Royal Bank built up a very large holding
of Bank of Scotland notes and then suddenly presented them
all – at the same time. Their judgement was that their rivals
could not possibly honour them. At first the strategy worked,
and in March 1728 the Old Bank, as it was known, was forced
to suspend payments and call in all its loans. This damaged
credibility and confidence badly, a circumstance banks abhor.
And the Royal Bank hoped that customers would migrate to
them in droves. But the Old Bank recovered and was able to
begin redeeming its notes with interest, and six months later
it resumed lending. To ensure that this ploy could not be
repeated, in either direction, the two rivals added an 'optional
clause' that allowed them, in return for interest, to delay
payment for as long as six months. Eventually a truce was
agreed, but it was not until 1751 that the Royal Bank of
Scotland and the Bank of Scotland agreed to accept each
other's notes.

Three years before peace broke out, a third bank was
founded in Edinburgh. Formed in 1746 to promote and
support linen manufacture in Scotland, the British Linen
Bank opened offices at Tweeddale Court, down a close off the
High Street. So that linen makers all over Scotland could
have easier access to their services and negotiate credit, the
new bank pioneered the opening of branches. The Commercial
Bank of Scotland in 1810 and the National Bank of Scotland
in 1815 both opened for business in Edinburgh, and all of
them issued their own notes. By the twentieth century, at
least six banks in Scotland were printing their own notes: the
Bank of Scotland, the Royal Bank of Scotland, the British
Linen Bank, the Commercial Bank, the National Bank of
Scotland and the Clydesdale Bank in Glasgow all made
money more colourful, and bemused English visitors. In

1959 the National Commercial Bank was the result of a merger between the Commercial Bank and the National Bank of Scotland, and the British Linen Bank became part of the Bank of Scotland in 1971.

The worldwide reputation of Edinburgh's banks for probity and caution was shattered in 2008. The Royal Bank's ancient, aggressive instincts resurfaced when Fred Goodwin became chief executive in 2001. He and his board embarked on a dizzying cycle of acquisition, taking over the much bigger English bank of NatWest and a string of smaller American financial institutions. In a very short time, the Royal Bank's assets quadrupled, and at first its profits soared. Leaving behind the solidity and tradition embodied by its glorious Georgian headquarters in St Andrew Square, the bank built a vast new £350 million centre at Gogarburn, not far from Edinburgh Airport. People joked that RBS, as it came to be known, wasn't so much a Scottish bank; it was more that Scotland was a country attached to a bank.

In 2007 Goodwin and his board bought the Dutch bank, ABN AMRO, using up a huge proportion of its cash reserves, and RBS briefly became the largest bank in the world with assets of £2.2 trillion, larger than Britain's GDP. But very quickly it all began to unravel. Many of the recent acquisitions were riddled with rotten debt that would have to be written off. Driven by greed, by bonuses and high salaries, executives had gambled in what they called, euphemistically, the 'sub-prime' markets, loans on property to people who did not have the means to pay them back, people who would probably have been refused loans in the past. So long as property values rose, the risks were less. But in 2007 these values in the USA began to stall and set off a chain reaction that led to bankruptcy for RBS and several other British banks. The British government was forced to step in and bail out these institutions by buying controlling shares and injecting vast amounts of cash to maintain services to their customers. The rescue has cost British taxpayers billions, much of which will never be repaid. Another shift took place as a consequence of all this. Most Edinburgh financial institutions are now essentially branch offices. For the reality is that the reputation of banking in Edinburgh and across the world will take a long time to recover.

21

Disunion

Historians have argued that it was the financial ruin caused by the failure of the Darien Scheme that forced the Union of the Scottish and English Parliaments in 1707. In the late 1690s the Company of Scotland was created by an Act of Parliament passed in Edinburgh, and it attracted a huge amount of investment, perhaps 20 per cent of all the cash in circulation, much of it from institutions and individuals in the city. The proposal was to colonise part of what is now Panama and establish an overland route between the Atlantic and the Pacific. It was a sound strategy disastrously executed with great loss of life and a total loss of all the cash invested. At the end of the seventeenth century, Scotland was suddenly close to bankruptcy. Coupled with that total failure was a series of bad harvests. Known as the Seven Ill Years, there was widespread famine (mainly due to bad and unseasonably cold weather) and perhaps 15 per cent of the population died of starvation. There were four failed harvests in 1695, 1696, 1698 and 1699. Others believe that the Union was the result of sustained politicking by those aristocrats who stood to benefit. One thing is certain: Edinburgh did not like it, and the people of Edinburgh in particular loathed what was proposed.

For a variety of dynastic and foreign policy reasons the English Parliament passed the Alien Act of 1705. This threatened to impoverish Scotland by ending the duty-free trade with England and also, incidentally, removing the automatic right of all Scots to English citizenship (and vice versa). The Alien Act would come into force unless the Scots accepted the Hanoverian succession and agreed to begin negotiations on parliamentary union. The Edinburgh mob was incensed, and when an English merchant ship had the ill fortune to seek shelter in Leith harbour, all hell broke loose. The captain, first mate and gunner were dragged off to jail, found guilty of piracy and hanged.

Nevertheless, negotiations did eventually begin. A Bill of Union was drawn up for the English Parliament in 1706, and, in essence, the Scots could either take it or leave it. There being only one realistic option, negotiators set out for London. In a building behind an old theatre, of all places, off Whitehall, the negotiators assembled but did not meet: the Scots sat in one room and the English in another, and they communicated in writing. Despite this, after only ten days, they had hammered out an agreement, detailing twenty-five articles of union. Almost all that remained was for the Scottish Parliament to approve it, or not.

Assurances were agreed over the independence of the Church of Scotland and the legal system, and large amounts of money changed hands, but there was little evidence of enthusiasm in England for the Union. It was a political necessity, nothing more.

The moment when Great Britain came into being was not 16 January 1707, when the Scottish Parliament voted itself out of existence by 110 votes to 67, or even when the Scots delegation delivered its consent to London. The events of the afternoon of 6 March 1707 were what turned the direction of history. Queen Anne, the last available Protestant member of the Stuart dynasty, came to parliament to sit on her throne in the House of Lords, and Black Rod banged on the door three times to summon the Commons into her presence. When all were assembled, the Clerk of the Crown read out the titles of eight bills to be given the royal assent and passed into law. Only four concerned public matters and they were: an Act of Union of the two kingdoms of England and Scotland; an Act for better preventing Escapes out of the Queen's Bench and Fleet prisons; an Act for repairing the Highway between Hockcliffe and Woodburn in the County of Bedford; and an Act . . . for repairing the Highways in the County of Hereford.

To see an epoch-making Act of Parliament given the same status as road repairs and measures to prevent convicts escaping lends some sort of historical perspective.

When the Scottish Parliament was formally dissolved in April 1707 and the Union came into effect a month later, Edinburgh wept. Having lost the royal court and now the parliament, it was no longer a capital city. The people rioted.

And Robert Burns was retrospectively outraged, writing the angry lines below. His poem about the dismal end to the Scottish Parliament is still sung – and to a dirge-like lament. Here is the last, doleful verse.

> O would, or I had seen the day
> That Treason thus could sell us,
> My auld grey head had lien in clay,
> Wi' Bruce and loyal Wallace!
> But pith and power, till my last hour,
> I'll mak this declaration;
> We're bought and sold for English gold –
> Such a parcel of rogues in a nation!

The Edinburgh mob made it their business to hunt down the parcel of treacherous rogues, and when the English government agent Daniel Defoe (author of *Robinson Crusoe*) made the mistake of looking out of the window of his lodgings at Moubray House in the High Street, he was recognised and pelted with stones and rubbish. The writer had only been curious about the source of the disturbance and later in a letter sniffed that a 'Scots rabble is the worst of its kind'.

22

Exotic Edinburgh

Robert Sibbald should be more celebrated. Educated at the Royal High School and a graduate of Edinburgh University, he was the very embodiment of a Renaissance man. He trained as a doctor and founded the Royal College of Physicians in Edinburgh and in 1685 was appointed the first Professor of Medicine at the university, where he established its unrivalled reputation for excellence and innovation. In 1682 he began work on something completely different, an updated and definitive atlas of Scotland. He wrote to parish ministers and local lairds to recruit them in this great project and was appointed Geographer Royal in 1682. Sibbald was also fascinated by whales and produced the first scientific study of the blue whale, the largest animal ever to have existed. It was usually known not as the blue whale but as Sibbald's rorqual.

Robert Sibbald's remarkable life and achievements may have faded from popular view since his death in 1722, but he has left a huge monument to his work in Edinburgh. It is not a statue or a plaque, but a garden, the beautiful Royal Botanic Garden, affectionately known in the city as 'the Botanics'.

With his friend, Andrew Balfour, also a doctor and an anti-quary, Sibbald was involved in the compilation of the *Edinburgh Pharmacopeia*, essentially a recipe book for making medicines. Since these were mostly plant-based, a supply of the right sort of herbs and other plants was needed. At St Anne's Yards, part of the ancient area of sanctuary around Holyrood Abbey – but now enclosed by a wall to the south of the palace; on the other side is the public car park in the Queen's Park – Sibbald and Balfour set up a physic garden. It was small, only about forty feet square, but with the help of plant collectors, they 'made a collection of eight or nine hundred plants'. Not surprisingly, the site proved to be too restricted, and the physic garden was moved to Trinity Hospital. Much later this was obliterated by the building of Waverley Station. A plaque on Platform 11 commemorates it.

In the early 1820s, the old physic garden expanded enormously when it moved from its location at the top of Leith Walk to a new site, what became the seventy acres of the Botanics on Inverleith Row. Where it has flourished ever since. Those who walk around the wonderful collection of outdoor plants (and entry is free, with only a small charge to get into the glasshouses) may not be aware that the garden is at the centre of a worldwide network of institutions seeking to limit the effects of climate change and other factors on the world's biodiversity. There are almost 273,000 plants growing at the Botanics and in its three satellite gardens at Dawyck in the Scottish Borders, Logan in Galloway and Benmore on the Cowal Peninsula. This comprises 4 per cent of all known plant species.

Robert Sibbald might have been most interested in the Herbarium. In this purpose-built facility there are about 3 million specimens, representing between a half and two thirds of the world's flora. The oldest specimen was collected in 1697, when Robert was still alive and, as ever, very active.

23

The Beast of Edinburgh

The eighteenth-century Edinburgh mob was very powerful. Drawn from the densely packed streets and closes of the Old Town, it could form in minutes. And the objects of the mob's anger found it difficult to escape. Judges who pronounced an unpopular verdict or a harsh sentence were often 'peebled', forced to suffer a pelting with pebbles, as they scurried home down a close off the High Street. Perhaps the occasional glance out of the windows of the Court of Session made for more circumspect justice.

A deeply unpopular judgement in 1736 ignited Edinburgh's most notorious bout of public disorder. The prelude was the hanging of Andrew Wilson on the scaffold in the Grassmarket, a preferred execution site because larger crowds could gather there than could squeeze into the High Street. He was a smuggler, but the crime which put a noose round Wilson's neck was theft; he had stolen goods from a customs officer. In the Court of Session Wilson argued that he had in fact been the victim and was only repossessing what was lawfully his. The customs officer had victimised him, repeatedly seizing his goods and ultimately rendering Wilson penniless. He had been forced to steal, he claimed. The judges did not believe him and handed down a death sentence. But the Edinburgh mob did, and after the execution, there was an outraged riot.

The City Guard was summoned and, under the command of Captain John Porteous, they greatly inflamed an already incendiary situation by firing on the crowd. Thirty were wounded or killed. The town council was forced to act, Porteous was quickly arrested and in his turn condemned to hang. Sir Walter Scott described the scene in the Grassmarket: 'The place of execution was crowded almost to suffocation . . . and resembled a huge, dark lake or sea of human heads, in the centre of which arose the fatal tree, tall, black and ominous, from which dangled the deadly halter.'

But the condemned man did not appear. No guards brought him down to the Grassmarket and rumours began to ricochet around the city. In fact, Porteous had petitioned Queen Charlotte (regent in place of her temporarily mad husband, George III), and a stay of execution had been granted, arriving in Edinburgh just in time. Trembling town magistrates announced this to the crowd, who immediately turned into a mob and took matters into their own hands. After the doors of the Tolbooth had been burned down, Porteous was dragged out and down to the Grassmarket, where he was strung up on a dyer's pole.

As a public space where the drama of raw politics played out, and sometimes to fatal effect, the centre of the city could be a cockpit. Crammed into David I's 143 acres, with soaring, tottering tenements more like rookeries than living spaces, were upwards of 57,000 people. That was the estimate of Alexander Webster, an Edinburgh minister who undertook the first serious attempt at a census in Scotland and whose charge was the Tolbooth Church in the High Street. That meant a population density of 600 people an acre, bearing in mind open spaces. There was no other city like it in Europe.

For about a hundred years a beast roamed the streets, wynds and closes of Edinburgh. The local constables, the City Guard, made themselves scarce when the beast roared. This was how the infamous Edinburgh mob was seen, a phenomenon as influential as that of ancient Rome. Because of the overcrowding of the tenements, the mob needed only to run down hundreds of stairs or up the wynds and closes from the Cowgate and the Grassmarket to assemble in the High Street in minutes. Politicians were powerless and judges were terrified of it. But the beast could be tamed, even led and influenced.

Sometime around 1750, an unlikely leader did emerge who could not only summon the beast onto the streets but could control it. He was a humble cobbler from the Cowgate with a grand but well-merited title – General Joe Smith. Because of a severe deformity caused by rickets, a common condition amongst the malnourished urban poor until the middle of the twentieth century, Smith was better known as Bowed Joseph. He was said to have been tiny and very over-bent. Nevertheless, he wielded real power and could gather the mob in a matter of minutes. When an issue or injustice came to his attention, Joseph picked up his drum and walked up and down the High Street banging it loudly. Ten thousand could be at his back in moments, and no power in the city could resist those numbers.

After a poor harvest, sometime in the 1760s, merchants were charging high prices for scarce oatmeal, a staple food for ordinary people. But before any could suffer, Joseph forced sellers to restrict their prices. And when one was found to be giving short measures, the drum sounded in the High Street. Not only was the merchant forced to deal out full measures, the beast ransacked his premises, his house as well as his shop. All the City Guard could do was watch – and keep their distance.

Such was Bowed Joseph's power, that even though he was unelected, the town council often deferred to him, encouraging him to mediate in disputes or broker a deal between parties. When he called out the beast, Joseph always insisted that the council pay for hogsheads of ale for them. His power was certainly not physical, and it probably derived from his honesty. There is no record of Joseph profiting from any of his activities, and he seems always to have acted in defence of others, of ordinary people. Perhaps he was charismatic, a gifted orator. The councillors will nevertheless have breathed a sigh of relief when he died in 1780, having fallen off a coach bringing him back to the Cowgate from Leith Races.

24

The Rookeries

In 1621 the town council forbade thatched roofs, insisting on slates or tiles. Too many fires had raged through Edinburgh when sparks had floated upwards and caught. And after 1674 no new wooden buildings on the street frontages were permitted. Thomas Gledstane's house in the Lawnmarket was built in the seventeenth century and it still stands in its original condition, now called Gladstone's Land (another name for a tenement). Not only does it have a well-made stone frontage, its arcading is also preserved. The town council had decreed that all the High Street shops should have arcades in front, but only one survives.

The towering, densely populated tenements of the Old Town could easily enclose a boiling cauldron of disorder such as the protests led by Bowed Joseph, and the town council increasingly found the city to be ungovernable. When the Porteous Riots brought censure from London, it was the town council, not the mob, who were forced to pay a fine of £2,000 (which went to the captain's widow).

In any case the burgesses had long been anxious to break out and expand Edinburgh. In 1716 the town council bought the land to the north, the fields beyond the Nor Loch known as Bearford's Parks. And to the south, the Burgh Loch was at last drained by a farmer and landowner who lived in a grand townhouse at the east end. Thomas Hope of Rankeillor (commemorated in Hope Park Terrace and Rankeillor Street) was given the lease of the boggy area of the loch, and he laid out footpaths drained by ditches on either side with lime trees planted along their length. The old loch drained to the west, into the Dalry Burn (appropriately at what is now Lochrin Place) and then ran into the Water of Leith at Roseburn. Its course has long since disappeared under the city.

As the eighteenth century wore on, the town council real-ised that Edinburgh had to expand beyond the Flodden Wall. Continuing upwards growth was neither feasible nor safe. After the devastating fire of 1676, Robertson's Land had been built, rising to a giddy fourteen storeys between the Cowgate and Parliament Square. It was completed in 1684 but only stood for sixteen years until fire ripped through the rookeries of the Old Town once more. Other buildings sometimes suffered partial collapse, losing a gable end, roofs caving in, and the city seemed almost organic – like an ant heap. A map of 1724 shows an astonishing 337 closes and pends leading off the spinal streets of the Lawnmarket, the High Street and the Canongate. By 1984 there were only 110, and 18 of those were closed to public access.

The legal and mercantile classes of Old Town Edinburgh had long lived a dense, intense version of urban life, full of stark contrasts. While they dined in elegant rooms in the vast tenements, people far down the social scale lived in tiny, filthy hovels reached by the same stairway. In Old Assembly Close, only a few yards from the dank cells of Tolbooth prison and the brothels and drinking dens of the Cowgate, a strange, repressed form of social intercourse took place. The dancing assemblies, as they were known, were sterile, starchy affairs. The sexes were permitted to dance, very formally, in sets, but only under the stern gaze of Miss Nicky Murray, the Lady Directress of the 1750s, and they were most certainly not allowed to mix. Men on one side, young ladies on the other. Oliver Goldsmith, the novelist, observed that there was no more intercourse between the sexes than between two countries at war. Only one set was allowed on the dance floor at any one time, and in this ritual-like atmosphere few were able to dance more than once. At one end of the Assembly Room, Miss Murray sat on a high chair raised on a dais, no doubt vigilant for any impropriety.

Meanwhile, outside in the High Street, it was not unusual, according to the Edinburgh chronicler Robert Chambers to see some very different sights: 'Nothing was so common in the morning as to meet men of high rank and dignity reeling home from a close in the High Street where they had spent the night in drinking.'

Drunks who could afford it were sometimes escorted through the streets and closes by caddies, the name adopted for a very different role in golf. Not only could they interpret the vague directions waved at by a wealthy inebriate, they could also fend off any who wished to relieve their charge of his cash and valuables. These men and boys were themselves described as a ragged, half-blackguard-looking set, but they had a sound reputation for honesty and dependability. Many of them were Highlanders. Holding up a storm lantern, the caddies not only led drunks back up their closes and stairs to their front doors and what was surely waiting behind them, they also acted as messengers and bearers. Caddies appear to have acted as an informal but effective police force, and an eighteenth-century English observer believed that they were the reason why there was less theft and housebreaking in Edinburgh than anywhere else. The impression is of native guides in an urban jungle.

Indoors similarly primitive social practices might have raised a modern eyebrow. Even in the grand flats of the Old

Town the sanitary arrangements were often somewhat sketchy. Sewage and dirty water had probably not been tipped into the street out of upper-floor windows (with the cry 'gardyloo', meaning 'Watch out for the water!'), at least not since the Middle Ages, but eighteenth-century plumbing had not quite taken over. Under the sideboard in many dining rooms sat a chamber pot, and one of the persuasive reasons why the ladies were in the habit of withdrawing to the withdrawing room was to allow the gentlemen to use it – without a break in the conversation. The drinking culture (claret, of course, being the preferred tipple) of the Old Town was legendary. Male guests often slid off their chairs in the dining room as they literally drank themselves under the table. One was roused from his stupor, appalled, because he thought he was being strangled. 'But I'm just the laddie that looses the cravats,' said his imagined assailant. Details such as this act as a surprising gloss on the candle-lit elegance of eighteenth-century Edinburgh society.

25

Tartan Town

In common with most of urban Scotland, such as it was in 1745, Edinburgh stayed loyal to the Hanoverian cause when Bonnie Prince Charlie raised the Highland clans in support of the Stewart claim on the throne. But at the approach of the rebel army, the defenders of the city proved useless. When flanking Jacobite cavalry encountered a force of government dragoons at Coltbridge, near Roseburn, there was a rout. In what was called the Canter of Coltbrig, the moment the soldiers saw the approach of the Highland army, they simply fled for their lives.

Church bells rang out in the city and the streets filled with panicking people. Sixteen thousand slavering Highland savages were said to be marching on Edinburgh, and they would pillage, burn, steal – and worse. Charles Mackie, Professor of History at the university, spread stories of Jacobite atrocities but, when challenged, cheerfully admitted that he had made them up, hoping to galvanise 'loyalist sentiment'. A force of University Volunteers mustered at the High School Yards but was eventually gently dissuaded by the principal from doing more than throwing their hats in the air and raising a few huzzas. Most of the students then marched up to the castle, which was (and remained) in the hands of a government garrison and gave their weapons to the soldiers so that they should not fall into enemy hands. It was suggested that regiments of women might be recruited who were 'willing to parry a thrust'. No one was sure exactly what that meant. Meanwhile Colin Maclaurin, Professor of Mathematics, ran frantically around the city walls trying to shore up breaches and emplace cannon. Few helped him.

A Jacobite commander, Lord Elcho, recorded what happened when the Highlanders halted outside the city:

At 8 o'clock at night the Prince sent a message to the magistrates of Edinburgh to demand the keys of the town and to tell them he intended to enter it either that night or the next day, and if there was any resistance made, whoever was found in arms should be severely treated; and besides, he could not answer but if the town was taken by storm his soldiers would plunder it. At ten at night there came four of the town council out to the Prince's quarters to beg he would give them time to think on his demand. This was a message contrived to gain time, for they expected General Cope's army every hour to land at Leith from Aberdeen, and in case he landed time enough, they intended to wait the event of a battle. The Prince, after they had kissed his hand, told them that he was going to send a detachment to attack the town and let them defend it at their peril; that if they did the consequences would be bad, and if they did not he intended no harm to the old metropolis of his kingdom. As soon as they received this answer the Prince ordered Young Locheil with 800 men to march and attack the town. There came out sometime after another deputation of six councillors; Provost Coutts was one of them. They got the same answer as the first, and the Prince did not see them. The coach that they came out in went in at the West Port and set down the company, and as they were letting out the coach at the Netherbow, Locheil's party who were arrived there rushed in, seized all the guards of the town, who made no resistance, and made themselves masters of Edinburgh without firing a shot.

In the event, Locheil's capture of the city provoked little violence on either side, and the Highlanders, who had camped between Holyroodhouse and Prestonfield House, appear to have behaved well. Prince Charles took up residence in the palace, and on 18 September at the Mercat Cross on the High Street, his father was proclaimed James VIII of Scotland and III of England, Wales and Ireland. A declaration that the Union of 1707 was dissolved was issued and published in the *Caledonian Mercury*, and Edinburgh briefly became a capital city once more.

The Highlanders had moved fast after their muster at Glenfinnan and out-manoeuvred General Cope's government army. Using General Wade's military road network, they had made their way down into the Lowlands unopposed. Cope's army took ship at Aberdeen and disembarked at Dunbar on 20 September before marching east to Prestonpans.

At dawn on the following morning, the clan regiments waited for the order to charge. In the hours before sunrise, they had marched around to the east of the government army. As the sea haar lifted, the war pipes skirled out the battle rants, and the Highlanders roared their war cries as they raced across the stubble fields. The wide-eyed redcoats, many of them raw recruits, had seen nothing like it. Clan Cameron smashed into their ranks first and immediately broke through. Panic rippled along the government lines, and men turned and fled, many without firing a shot, throwing down their weapons. The Battle of Prestonpans may have lasted little more than ten minutes. James Johnstone, the son of an Edinburgh merchant, had joined the Jacobite army, and his sense of shock is unmistakable: 'The field of battle presented a spectacle of horror, being covered with heads, legs, arms and mutilated bodies: for the killed all fell by the sword.'

The rout at Prestonpans horrified the London government and the Hanoverian king. At a stroke, Prince Charles had made himself master of Scotland, taking Edinburgh and destroying a government army. For some of the clan chiefs that was enough, and arguments about what should be done next raged at Holyroodhouse. The prince wished to invade England, to reclaim his whole kingdom for his father. That strategy prevailed, but although the Highlanders reached Derby, only 120 miles from London, where there was a degree of panic, it became clear that victory was unlikely. Too few English Jacobites had joined, and the French had made no move across the Channel, and so on the evening of 6 December, the Highlanders set out on the long march north, the long march into history.

On 16 April 1746 the prince's army was blown to pieces by a disciplined military barrage on Culloden Moor, and the dream of a Jacobite restoration vanished into the darkness of the past. But it did not seem like that to one young observer. Watching the battle on horseback from the south side of the moor, where the ground slopes away a little, he saw Clan Cameron break through the front ranks of the government army on their left wing, just as they had done at Prestonpans. But he had no view of what was happening beyond them. It seemed that the undefeated Highland charge had prevailed, as it had in all the battles of the rebellion. The young observer turned his horse southwards, and upon eventually arriving in Edinburgh, he reported another victory for the prince. But Jacobite celebrations were short-lived as news of what actually happened reached the city.

The last act of the 1745 rising took place some weeks later.

Edinburgh's public hangman walked down from the castle, leading a group of sooty chimney sweeps. Each carried a clan banner captured at Culloden. Usually, enemy colours were preserved and displayed as trophies, but orders had been sent from London that these symbols of rebellion, some of them saltires, should be utterly extirpated, like the witches a century and a half before. At the Mercat Cross, the hangman burned the silk banners of the Highland army, and as their smoke floated above the rooftops of the Old Town, an older vision of Scotland began to disappear.

26

Bearford's Parks

After the smoke had cleared at Culloden, and the prince had long since fled, Edinburgh began to look to its future. Lord Provost George Drummond put a proposal to the Convention of Royal Burghs in 1752 for 'Carrying out Certain Public Works' in the city of Edinburgh, which contained the rallying cry: 'Let us boldly enlarge Edinburgh to the utmost.' At last.

Some urgency was injected into this stately process when the side wall of an Old Town tenement suddenly collapsed. Rooms on all six storeys were exposed, and the building had to be pulled down. Other rickety structures were examined, and to forestall another disaster, they too were demolished. Radical change was in the air; it was time to move forward.

Lord Provost Drummond announced a competition to find the best layout for a New Town to be built on the other side of the Nor Loch, on the land known as Bearford's Parks (also as Barefoot's Parks in some accounts). By 1767 a winner had been chosen, the twenty-three-year-old James Craig, and his simple three-street grid connecting two squares at either end was adopted. It used the ridge that ran from east to west across Bearford's Parks and the gentle inclines on the northern and southern flanks. Work began immediately, and the foundations for the first houses were dug at what is now Thistle Court in Thistle Street, just off St Andrew Square.

Craig's plan resembled a political diagram. The street names were a self-conscious affirmation of the Hanoverian succession and the Act of Union as well as a rejection of the Stewart dynasty and the recent rebellion of 1745–46. George Street was named for George III and was of course the principal, axial street intended to run along the parks' ridge. It was to connect St Andrew Square with St George's Square – but an immediate difficulty arose. In what was, by a whisker, Edinburgh's first new development to follow Provost Drummond's declaration, George Square had been laid out on the south side of the city in 1766. It was not named after the saint or the mad king but the architect's brother. A compromise was reached, and Queen Charlotte (almost the saviour of Captain Porteous) was thought to be much pleased to have the western square of the New Town renamed after her.

On either side of George Street, symbolising the Act of Union, lay Rose Street and Thistle Street. To the north was Queen Street, and to the south James Craig had marked the track known as the Lang Dykes as St Giles Street. But the king would have none of it and insisted that St Giles Street be changed and named for his sons, the Duke of York and the Duke of Rothesay. Princes Street was the result, and the first house was built at the east end in 1769.

Edinburgh's New Town was the largest example of urban planning in eighteenth-century Britain. Intended as a residential suburb, much of the central area has been adapted for retail and business use, but 75 per cent of the whole, expanded New Town is still stubbornly used for housing. Princes Street had shops from the outset, and when construction reached the west end in 1805, many of the new buildings had been designed as shops. There was an early attempt to have buildings on both sides of Princes Street, but a group of influential

Edinburgh residents argued down the plan. An early outing for what would become a powerful middle-class conservationist lobby.

Craig's layout did not quite work, especially at its east and west ends. Designed as a direct link between the Old Town and the New, North Bridge began construction in 1765. It should have connected directly with St Andrew Square, which in turn should have been built a little further to the east. But Edinburgh's town council had not been able to acquire the land just below Calton Hill. The circumstances of ownership were not clear, but it looks as though Sir Laurence Dundas had bought land in that location and before Craig's plan was published he had decided on a grand house. Until recently it was the head office of the Royal Bank of Scotland. More complications were on the way. Dundas then acquired the plot of land immediately to the west of his new house, along the street line of St Andrew Square, as Craig had laid it out. It became the entrance to the house and its garden. Either side of it two identical and beautifully proportioned flanking buildings give the impression of a country house with wings around a central forecourt in front of what is the only free-standing mansion in the New Town. Together the scheme achieves an overall impression of considerable style. But for the town council it was a considerable headache. Dundas' single-mindedness seriously upset the symmetry of Craig's plan. To finish the eastern vista along George Street, he had intended to place St Andrew's Church in St Andrew Square. Another much less satisfactory site had to be found on the line of George Street.

Halfway along Princes Street the Mound was slowly rising. After the Nor Loch had been drained, the town council ordered that all the earth dug out of the foundations of the New Town's terraces ought to be piled up to create a land bridge linking the bottom of the Lawnmarket with the new development. But once again there were problems. The roads did not quite connect, there being an awkward wiggle between the foot of the Mound and Hanover Street.

Further west Craig's rectilinear layout had to incorporate another snag. The line of the old road to South Queensferry (now Queensferry Street) ran north-west, at an angle from the Lang Dykes. When Hope Street attempted to link Charlotte Square with Princes Street, an unfortunate hairpin turn had to be allowed for as well as the junction with the foot of Lothian Road. It was a mess only recently sorted out by continuing the Princes Street pavement to Shandwick Place and separating the two competing traffic flows.

Once building work had begun at Thistle Court in 1767, the town council hoped that plots would be quickly snapped up. But the New Town took time to become fashionable, and while James Craig's layout was to be strictly adhered to (by everyone except Sir Laurence Dundas), the regulations for housebuilding were at first not so rigorous. It may be that the town council felt that too many restrictions might discourage buyers. All they insisted on were three-storey terraced houses with sunk basements, usually accessible from a small lower ground-floor forecourt. Early variations in design are clear on the north side of St Andrew Square, where some houses are faced with smooth ashlar, others with rubble-cut stone, while the windows are either architraved or plain.

By the time gangs of masons and their labourers reached Charlotte Square, demand had grown and the New Town had become a much sought-after address. And a masterpiece was created. Designed by Robert Adam in 1791, Charlotte Square was to have no variations in the terraced houses – instead the north and south sides were to mirror each other precisely with severe but impressive and unifying classical temple façades.

Nothing as monumental had yet been built in the New Town. Adam's central notion was to plan coherent façades on the theme of a Roman temple but to have eleven three-storey houses behind each one. This time no wealthy developer was allowed to bully his way in, and to finish the western vista along George Street and to occupy much of the western side of the square, St George's Church was built. The result is perhaps the most beautiful Georgian square in Britain. And it has been carefully preserved in every detail; the mysterious rectangular stone blocks on the edge of the pavements were a classical version of what Scots-speaking horsemen still call a 'loupin on stane'.

27

Old Town Down

In 1760 more than 70,000 people crammed into the tenements of the Old Town, and the temptation for the genteel (who generally lived on the middle and upper floors) was to seek to live in 'houses to themselves' in the New Town. As building work gathered pace and Craig's plan took shape, the wealthier citizens began to migrate in numbers across the Nor Loch to live in spacious terraced houses with their own front door and without the need to hold their noses as they passed 'undesirables' on the tenement stair. In fact 'the Great Flitting' became an entertainment for the undesirables, and as the affluent packed their furniture, crockery and carpets onto carts, they came out to see them off as they clattered down the Mound to another life.

Most cities are composed of connected villages, more or less salubrious neighbourhoods, and the Great Flitting saw Edinburgh begin to divide along these lines. The rickety medieval ant heap not only lost its wealthier citizens but also a real sense of community. The fact of poor people living on the same stair as the rich and powerful, of people seeing close-up how other, very different lives were lived, of simply talking to each other regularly – all of this appears very attractive now, in an alienated, fragmented urban world.

As the carts rattled away over the cobbles, those who were left in the Old Town enjoyed some dividends. The memory and novelty of these were still fresh in the nineteenth century when an old lady recounted the pleasures of high living in a house in Carrubber's Close, off the High Street, which had been vacated by Lord Elphinstone:

> Talk about chimney-pieces – it was the nicest, sweetest thing you ever saw: lovely bunches of grapes, all carved like real, and fruit in baskets and flowers all growing about. Oh my, it was a bonny place to be in! . . . I used to buy beeswax for the mantel and always spend a good two hours on it on Saturday doing it up. It was bonny – bonny to be in a house like that.

Airs and graces began to float over the rooftops of the New Town as the new residents moved in. Instead of hard-drinking nights in the 'howffs' or public houses of the Old Town and early morning staggers up the High Street on the arm of a caddie, the refined pleasures of dancing assemblies were introduced to George Street. On the occasion of the Caledonian Hunt Ball on 11 January 1787, the Assembly Rooms opened. The grand ballroom was lit by 'crystal lustres' and down its impressive length the strictly segregated sexes joined in sets and reels. There was to be 'no admission without a ticket on any account whatever'. As they stepped along George Street, clutching their tickets, some of the new New Town residents may have cast a longing glance up to the canyons of the Old Town and their warm and friendly howffs down the closes and pends. In more senses than the architectural, Edinburgh would never be the same again.

The population of Edinburgh had begun to increase rapidly by the end of the eighteenth century. In 1791 it was estimated that 90,000 lived in the city; by 1860 that number had mushroomed to 220,000. As farms became larger and more efficient, Scots began to leave the land and migrate to the towns and cities. And the Highland Clearances began to force people south. The Industrial Revolution had created huge mills, factories and foundries where migrants could find work. Housing was often more problematic, and in Edinburgh's Old Town the tenements vacated by the better-off were divided and sub-divided to cram more and more people into them. Sanitation did not improve, and the city saw regular outbreaks of cholera and typhoid that killed thousands of citizens.

On 15 November 1824, a fire broke out in the tenements in Old Assembly Close, not far from St Giles and on the same side of the street. Only two months before, the Edinburgh Fire Brigade had been formed, and it was quickly on the scene. But no usable source of water could be found in time, and the blaze took hold, fanned by the wind, ripping through the tenements all the way down to the Tron Kirk. The steeple caught fire and molten lead dripped onto the cobbles. Buildings to the south, between the High Street and the Cowgate, also caught fire. Once James Braidwood, the leader of the Pioneers, the fire brigade, had located a source of water, they fought to defend St Giles from the flames, and its stonework suffered only scorching.

When the blaze finally subsided on 19 November, partly doused by persistent rain, dozens of tenements on the south side of the High Street were little more than charred ruins, the stark silhouettes of their blackened, roofless gables all that was left. The young David Octavius Hill, later to become a pioneer of modern photography, made accurate sketches of the damage. The Old Assembly Hall, the domain of the eagle-eyed Lady Directress Miss Nicky Murray, had been completely consumed, and between 400 and 500 families had lost their homes.

The dangerous ruins were quickly pulled down, and a programme of rebuilding began. The law courts in Parliament Square had also been defended by the fire brigade and they were extended, and on that side of the High Street a run of well-designed Georgian tenements was built, which can be seen above the modern shop, pub and restaurant frontages. Most of the building work was completed by 1829. Watching the blaze from the safe distance of the New Town, former residents must have had mixed feelings, but one thing was certain. Here is the view of the publisher, Robert Chambers:

> Edinburgh is in fact two towns in more ways than one. It contains an upper and under town – the one a sort of thoroughfare for the children of business and fashion, the other a den of retreat for the poor, the diseased and the ignorant.

28

Enlightened Edinburgh

In 1769 David Hume moved to a house in St David Street, off St Andrew Square. Having been librarian of the Advocates Library, secretary to several diplomats and a failed academic, Hume's principal claim to popular fame in eighteenth-century Edinburgh was his atheism. After a serious drinking session in the Old Town, the somewhat overweight Hume is said to have fallen into an undrained part of the Nor Loch as he weaved his way back to his new home. Unable to extricate himself without help, he appealed to a passing old lady. 'Ah!' she exclaimed. 'It's Hume the atheist.' She refused to pull him out of the bog until he had recited the Creed and the Lord's Prayer. Which of course he did.

David Hume is famous for other reasons. As one of the central figures of the Scottish Enlightenment, the extraordinary outpouring of scholarship, publishing and original thought which came principally from Edinburgh between 1760 and 1800, his reputation as a historian and philosopher is worldwide. Alongside him shone a galaxy of towering intellectual figures who advanced the understanding of many disciplines, from geology to medicine, from horticulture to aesthetics. Hume, William Robertson, Adam Ferguson, Lord Kames and dozens of other men of renown met in a series of clubs in the Old Town: the Poker, the Select and so on. Publications such as *Blackwood's Magazine* and the *Edinburgh*

Review carried articles and extracts, but perhaps the most famous literary product of the Scottish Enlightenment was first printed in Anchor Close, off the High Street. The *Encyclopaedia Britannica* became a world-famous standard.

The editor was William Smellie, and he began this monumental work in 1768. This was an age when the setting down of all human knowledge was thought possible – a listing of all there was to know. The great encyclopaedia appeared in 100 weekly instalments at a rate of about one every ten days until it was completed in 1771. Its entries could be pithy. The one for 'woman' was only four words long – 'the female of man'. But the encyclopaedia proved very popular, and a second edition was soon put in train.

The particular factors that produced this remarkable intellectual ferment known as the Scottish Enlightenment are difficult to describe – but one of the key circumstances which sustained it was the nature of Edinburgh's Old Town. Most of these great figures were near-neighbours and knew each other. They met regularly in the closes and the howffs. Discussion, ferocious argument, competition and cooperation forced the intellectual pace, and the production of innovative ideas was astonishing. Much of this was firmly rooted in practicality – and again Edinburgh's intense urban life had a strong influence. The old woman who helped David Hume out of the Nor Loch not only knew who he was, he also knew a great deal about her life.

John Amyatt was an English chemist who thought that Edinburgh was unique. On a visit to the city sometime in the 1770s, he remarked to William Smellie that the city 'enjoyed a noble privilege not possessed by any other in Europe'. It was not the views out to the Firth of Forth, or the magnificent location of the castle he was referring to, but the intellectual excitement of the Enlightenment at its zenith. When Smellie asked Amyatt to elaborate, he replied: 'Here I stand at what is called the Cross of Edinburgh, and can in a few minutes, take 50 men of genius by the hand.'

It was nothing less than the truth. Scholars, lawyers, doctors, academics, writers, landowners, poets, painters and architects in Edinburgh, and also in Glasgow, Aberdeen and across Scotland had begun to articulate ideas that would change the way in which the world was understood. Without exaggeration, the men met by John Amyatt in the High Street, and many others, laid the foundations of modern society.

The seeds of this extraordinary flowering were planted in the Reformation of the sixteenth century, in the Magdalen Chapel in the Cowgate by the Six Johns and the necessity for the priesthood of all believers to be literate, for a school in every parish and a college in every town. Nevertheless, they would have been appalled at where their idealism had led – the formation of liberal ideas, and the atheism of David Hume, only temporarily suspended when the old fishwife pulled him out of the Nor Loch.

The Union of 1707 also had an impact. With the departure of the court and then the parliament to London, Scotland's remaining institutions, based in Edinburgh, began to flourish. A talented middle class formed, sometimes energised and refreshed by men from humble backgrounds who had seized the opportunities offered by parish schooling. In the overcrowded, relatively small area of the Old Town, these lawyers, writers, academics, artists and ministers knew each other. In the same way as the hothouse intensity of city life had allowed intellectual and artistic achievement to blossom in Athens, Rome and Florence, new thinking began to pour out of Edinburgh in particular.

David Hume was one of the greatest figures of the Enlightenment. Perhaps motivated by his inner struggles with what sounds like depression (one of his therapies was the daily consumption of a pint of claret), he began to consider what he thought of as the science of man. Published in 1739, *A Treatise of Human Nature* set out his reasons for believing that desire rather than reason governed the behaviour of human beings. Ideas were not innate, and people only had real knowledge of things they had directly experienced. Hume concluded that humans have no actual concept of self, but are aware only of a bundle of sensations or feelings associated with the self. Ethics, he argued, are based on those feelings and not on any set of moral principles. David Hume's work was enormously influential on figures as diverse as Albert Einstein and Immanuel Kant. The great German philosopher, Arthur Schopenhauer wrote: 'there is more to be learned from each page of David Hume than from the collected philosophical works of Hegel, Herbert and Schleiermacher taken together'.

Publishing also brightened the intellectual climate. In 1763 there were six printer-publishers and three paper mills in Edinburgh, but only twenty years later, sixteen printer-publishers were buying paper from twelve mills. The clubs were also cauldrons of gossip and cockpits of debate. The Select Society met in the Advocates Library, and its members included David Hume, Adam Smith, Allan Ramsay, the founder, and William Robertson. It gave way to the Poker Club, which had nothing to do with pokers for fires, but existed 'to poke things up a bit'. There were many others, but all of them seem to have involved lavish dinners and the consumption of a great deal of claret, an Edinburgh tradition. The Speculative Society still exists, meets regularly in the city, and it may be that some claret is drunk.

29

The Four Lives of Deacon Brodie

The wait must have been agonising, interminable. As the bells of St Giles tolled, the condemned men stood by the gallows on the platform outside the Tolbooth as the hangman adjusted the length of the ropes – three times. The vast crowd of 40,000 hushed when at last the nooses were tightened around the necks of William Brodie and George Smith. They had come in their droves to see how the mighty, or at least the respectable, would fall. And then the crowd gasped when the stools were kicked away and both men choked to death, their legs flailing, their faces turning purple.

It was 1 October 1788, and the end of an extraordinary story. William Brodie was a prosperous pillar of the mercantile middle classes in Edinburgh. Trained as a cabinetmaker and a locksmith, and taking over his father's established business, he lived and worked in Brodie's Close, off the Lawnmarket. Successful and apparently well liked, Brodie was elected deacon of the craft guild known as the Incorporation of Wrights, or woodworkers. They controlled the trade, apprenticeships and other aspects of business. As the deacon of a guild, William Brodie was entitled to sit on Edinburgh's town council, and his status ensured that he socialised at the highest levels. He met the great poet, Robert Burns, and the great painter, Sir Henry Raeburn. A member of a dining club (the Edinburgh Cape Club, which has recently been revived) whose members wore capes and took knightly names, Brodie, or Sir Llyud, seemed to be part of the establishment.

But he was not all he appeared to be. Brodie was in fact much more. What led him to the gallows was a double, triple, even quadruple life. He had five children with Mrs Brodie and five more with two mistresses, Anne Grant and Jean Watt. Neither mistress knew of each other's existence, and Brodie's wife had no idea of either. Effectively, Brodie had three families all living within a few hundred yards of each other in the Old Town. One can only admire his energy. But it was his fourth life that made all the others possible.

Whenever Brodie fitted a new lock to a door behind which valuables might be kept, he made an impression of the key on wax or putty, and had a duplicate produced. He kept his cache of copied keys hidden under a stone at the foot of Salisbury Crags. In 1768 he duplicated the keys to a bank and stole £800, a huge sum for the times and enough to keep three households going for a long period, to say nothing of funding the deacon's gambling habit. A pre-eminent locksmith in the city, Brodie worked for wealthy clients, whom he then robbed. By 1768 he had recruited John Brown, a convicted thief on the run from a sentence of transportation, and George Smith, an English locksmith who also kept a grocer's shop in the Cowgate. With a business to run during the day, three families with ten children to maintain and a legitimate social life to keep up, it may be that Brodie felt he needed help.

It all came to a very sticky end on 5 March 1788. Brodie led an armed robbery on the Excise Office in the Canongate, a government office for the collection of taxes. The raiders were disturbed but managed to escape. The following day, Smith and another member of the gang were arrested, and

Brodie realised that the game was up. He fled Edinburgh but was finally tracked down and arrested in Amsterdam. At the trial, John Brown turned King's Evidence against William Brodie and George Smith, and the judge handed down a death sentence for both men.

Fascinated by the story, Robert Louis Stevenson wrote a play, *Deacon Brodie, or the Double Life*, which eventually morphed into the famous novella, *The Strange Case of Dr Jekyll and Mr Hyde*. And in a curious addition to Deacon Brodie's literary legacy, Muriel Spark had Miss Jean Brodie claim to be a descendant. She too lived multiple lives.

30

Book Town

In 1507 James IV granted a charter, a monopoly, to Walter Chepman and Andrew Myllar to found a printing press in Edinburgh, the first in Scotland. The royal largesse had a price. The king would tell Chepman and Myllar what to print and publish: 'bukis [books] of our laws, actis of parliament, croniclis [chronicles], mess bukis [mass books] and portuus [breviaries] efter the use of our Realme, with addiciouns and legendis of Scottis sanctis [saints]'. And more than that, the king would decide what reasonable prices for these 'bukis' should be. Chepman and Myllar duly set up in the Cowgate but their business lasted only two or three years. However, it did mark the beginning of a long, often honourable and occasionally profitable tradition of printing and publishing in Edinburgh.

By the end of the eighteenth century, much stimulated by the ferment of the Enlightenment, printing and publishing had become an industry in the city. Improvements in technology improved output and quality as well as depressing costs. Charles Stanhope, an English aristocrat, invented the iron printing press, a tremendous advance because little had changed in the three centuries since Gutenberg. By the early nineteenth century Stanhope had developed a screw press that could apply consistent pressure on the paper over a large area, allowing several pages to be printed at once. The new press was eagerly adopted in Edinburgh, and just in time.

In 1795 Archibald Constable opened a bookshop in the High Street, not far from the Mercat Cross, and very quickly became involved in publishing, as many booksellers did. An advocate who often appeared at the nearby Court of Session brought Constable a collection of poetry he had made on his travels around the Tweed and Teviot Valleys and in the Cheviot Hills. Would Constable consider publishing it? After a modest but encouraging start, selling 800 copies in six months, *The Minstrelsy of the Scottish Border* became Sir Walter Scott's first success, and it launched him on a literary career that was epoch-making in many senses.

At first Scott's increasing fame rested on his long narrative poems. *The Lay of the Last Minstrel* became a bestseller, and Stanhope's iron press turned out thousands of copies for a growing readership. *Marmion* followed, and for it Constable paid Scott a substantial advance of 1,000 guineas. Sales were excellent: 8,000 copies were bought in 1808. Two years later, *The Lady of the Lake* did even better, selling 20,000 copies in one year. These were unprecedented numbers, and the scale of Scott's success encouraged others, both writers and publishers. But what really set the seal on a revolution was the reception of *Waverley*, Scott's first novel. First published anonymously in 1814, it took as its subject and setting the 1745 Jacobite Rebellion and went through six editions in two years. No fewer than twenty-six novels followed (as well as history and biography) as Scott and Constable invented the bestseller and Edinburgh established itself as the publishing – and printing – capital of Britain. Such was the sophistication and high quality of their output, printers such as Pillans & Wilson were used by London publishers who got into the habit of sending manuscripts north for typesetting, printing and binding.

Boom eventually turned to spectacular bust. By 1825 Archibald Constable had over-extended himself, and an early version of a credit crunch rendered him bankrupt. Scott had a financial interest in the business and suddenly found himself burdened with huge debts. But instead of accepting the stigma of bankruptcy, he promised to pay all he owed in full. 'Mine own right hand will do it,' Scott declared as he wrote and wrote, his popularity still strong, to publish as much as possible to clear all his obligations. He succeeded, but his herculean efforts broke the great man's health, and he died in 1832. It was not only his fame and talent that persuaded admirers to raise the huge Scott Monument in Princes Street and to name the city's central railway station, uniquely, after his first novel, but also his reputation for probity and decency. And a recognition that more than anyone, before or since, Scott had put Edinburgh and Scotland on the cultural map of Britain as well as Europe and North America.

Since those heady days of worldwide success in both publishing and printing, Edinburgh's place on the literary map has become less prominent. Only two major publishers now operate in the city. At Tweeddale Court, off the High Street, is the main entrance to the offices of Canongate Books, a very successful company also with offices in London. Above the door the name of a publishing predecessor, Oliver & Boyd, is engraved. It is pleasing to see continuity of that sort. In the south side of the city are the offices of Birlinn Limited, another very successful and prolific publisher with an unparalleled backlist of Scottish titles. Sir Walter Scott would have applauded, and Walter Chepman and Andrew Myllar would have smiled.

31

New New Town

When he had charge of the Advocates Library, David Hume would have been well aware of what a mess Scotland's national archives were in, with bundles of uncatalogued papers rotting in the Laigh Hall (under Parliament Hall) and in stores in the castle. They turned out to be an opportunity for Robert Adam to make another striking contribution to Edinburgh architecture. In 1771 he drew up plans for Register House. It was to be sited at the northern end of North Bridge and paid for by cash from forfeited Jacobite estates. The result is triumphant: the earliest purpose-built archive in Europe, and perhaps the most perfectly proportioned public building in Edinburgh. With New Register House behind, it still functions as the deposit for records of Scotland's births, marriages and deaths.

The memory of Edinburgh is often found in its street names. Heriot Row, the beautiful one-sided terrace to the north of Queen Street Gardens, is so called because the land on which it and most of the northern New Town was built belonged to George Heriot's Hospital. James Craig's original scheme had eventually proved so popular that demand grew for an extension, and the Heriot's Trust was persuaded to sell the land to the north of Bearford's Parks. It was crossed by Gabriel's Road, an old track leading from Register House down to the Water of Leith, to where it loops north towards Inverleith Park.

Very reminiscent of Craig's original, the grid plan has of course completely obliterated the old road, and it is laid out in a rectangle of streets stretching from Broughton Street in the east to India Street in the west. Designed for a hillside site by Robert Reid and William Sibbald in 1801–2, the northern New Town is a deftly managed development, all of which was built at approximately the same time. Its consequent architectural coherence is striking. Laid out on either side of broad Great King Street, the scheme connects London Street and Drummond Place with Royal Circus. It was a happy accident that land became available to the north of the first New Town because Craig's plan did not allow for immediate expansion in any other direction. Charlotte and St Andrew Squares had no exits on the western and eastern sides respectively. Only to the north could there be direct connection – from North St Andrew Street to Dublin Street, from Hanover Street to Dundas Street and Frederick Street to Howe Street. The Georgian housing beyond the Nor Loch now dwarfed the area of the Old Town. The new New Town was and remains overwhelmingly residential with shops, cafés, pubs and restaurants concentrated in Howe Street and Dundas Street. The nature of the housing also reflects social strata, and of course the ability to pay. The grandest houses are on the higher ground; Great King Street and Heriot Row are closer to the original New Town. Further downhill is Cumberland Street with accommodation that is more modest, the rooms smaller and less well-lit since the streets are narrower.

When more expansion was planned to the north-west, a brilliant solution was found to get around the awkwardness of Craig's layout of Charlotte Square and the diagonal line of the old road to Queensferry behind it. In 1822 the Earl of Moray decided he would cash in on the property boom and sell thirteen acres of land between the square and the Water of Leith. James Gillespie Graham proposed Moray Place as the grandest space (the earl was to live at number 28) and made it a polygon linked to Heriot Row by Darnaway Street. To the south-west the plots around the oval shape of Ainslie Place were pegged out, and beyond it Randolph Crescent led to Queensferry Street. It is perhaps the most satisfying example of town planning in all of the New Town, and the grey severity of its general style is much softened by the trees in the gardens of Moray Place, Ainslie Place and Randolph Crescent. What is striking is the use of available space in a restricted location. Moray Place, Great King Street and Heriot Row may be amongst the most expensive addresses in Scotland, but they are all either terraced houses or flats, some of them reached by a common stair – although no residents are expected to share a communal toilet. In 2024 a five-bedroom flat in Moray Place was selling at £915,000, a terraced house in Heriot Row for £1.5 million and a five-bedroom flat in Great King Street was listed at £935,000. Bargains all.

Finishing the western vista from Calton Hill are the three spires of St Mary's Cathedral. It is the centrepiece of the western New Town. The cathedral began development along the line of Shandwick Place and off Queensferry Street. The beautifully built church was made possible by the lucrative sale of parcels of land from the Easter Coates estate by Sir Patrick Walker. His heirs, the Misses Walker, who lived in Easter Coates House (at one time the location of St Mary's Music School), in turn left his fortune to the Scottish Episcopal Church so that a cathedral could be built. Seen from Melville Street, the western New Town's axial street, their generosity is very pleasing.

32

The Dumbiedykes

A new language was invented in Edinburgh, but it is not spoken anywhere. At Craigside House, which stood to the south of Holyrood Road until its demolition in 1939, a remarkable man set up a school to teach children how to write clearly and with confidence, a course in the art of penmanship as well as instruction in grammar. In 1760 Thomas Braidwood was visited by Alexander Shirreff, a wealthy wine merchant from Leith. He explained that his son, Charles, was a deaf mute, but could Braidwood teach him how to write? It would allow the boy at least one means of communication.

Reluctant but intrigued, Braidwood agreed. But could it be done? The ten-year-old could not hear how letters or words sounded, only associate what he wrote with objects he could see: a bird, an apple and so on. More abstract concepts were very difficult without the ability to hear or speak. And so Braidwood invented a language.

Developing it out of what he called 'the combined system', the teacher codified the earliest version of British Sign Language. It was based on the use of the hands, the shapes the fingers made and how they were turned, placed and moved. For example the letter 'C' is made by curving the thumb and index finger into a semi-circle, 'D' by adding the straight index finger of the other hand to the semi-circle.

Braidwood also taught the children who came to Craigside House how to lip-read.

In October 1773 the school had another visitor. Samuel Johnson was touring Scotland and rarely impressed. But when he went to meet Braidwood and his pupils, he left an extended note in his journal: _

There is one subject of philosophical curiosity to be found in Edinburgh, which no other city has to show; a college of the deaf and dumb, who are taught to speak, to read, and to write, and to do arithmetic, by a gentleman, whose name is Braidwood. The number which attends him is, I think, about twelve, which he brings together in a little school, and instructs according to their several degrees of proficiency.

... the improvement of Mr Braidwood's pupils is wonderful. They not only speak, write and understand what is written, but if he that speaks looks towards them, and modifies his organs [Johnson may mean lips here] by distinct and full utterance, they know so well what is spoken, that it is an expression scarcely figurative to say, they hear with the eye.

This school I visited, and found some of the scholars waiting for their master, whom they are said to receive at his entrance with smiling countenance and sparkling eyes, delighted with the hope of new ideas. One of the young ladies had her slate before her, on which I wrote a question consisting of three figures, to be multiplied by two figures. She looked upon it, and quivering her fingers in a manner which I thought very pretty, but of which I know not whether it was art or play [it was sign language, Samuel], multiplied the sum regularly in two lines, observing the decimal place; but did not add the two lines together, probably disdaining so easy an operation. I pointed at the place where the sum total should stand, and she noted it with such expedition as seemed to show that she had it only to write.

It was pleasing to see one of the most desperate of human calamities capable of so much help; whatever enlarges hope, will exalt courage; after having seen the deaf taught arithmetic, who would be afraid to cultivate the Hebrides?

The young woman baffled Johnson as she talked in a mesmerising flurry of hand movements. British Sign Language has developed regional dialects. Some Scottish signs are not understood in the south of England. Thomas Braidwood would have smiled to see BSL recognised alongside English, Welsh, Gaelic and others as one of Britain's official languages. And also to see that Dumbie House, the nickname for his original school at Craigside House, was passed on to the district around it, what became known as the Dumbiedykes.

33

The Kiltie King

In 1822 the great and the good in Edinburgh gathered at a royal levee at Holyrood Palace. Invitations were no doubt eagerly sought but must have caused some consternation. What to wear, how to behave? No one was sure since no reigning monarch had visited Scotland since Charles II in 1651, and he didn't stay long. Since the Hanoverian accession in 1714, none of the successive Georges had made the trip north, perhaps discouraged by the frequency of Jacobite Rebellions and the tartan-swathed savages who had cut a government army to pieces at Prestonpans. Sir Walter Scott was involved in stage-managing the visit and to assuage anxieties about etiquette and dress code, he issued a booklet: 'HINTS addressed to the INHABITANTS OF EDINBURGH AND OTHERS'. Those gentlemen attending levees were advised to wear a full dress suit and ladies to wear their finest gowns. All would be well!

At the Holyrood occasion, the suitably attired guests were silenced, perhaps even struck dumb by a remarkable entrance. Emerging through doors opened by footmen, swathed from head to foot in tartan, King George IV joined his subjects. Wearing two belts (to restrain his belly – he tipped the scales at twenty stone but was only a little over five feet tall), dirks, pistols and a bonnet, his kilt sat well above the knee over flesh-coloured tights, essential to hide his varicose veins. It may be that his belly was actually visible below the hem of his Royal Stuart kilt. Perhaps there were gasps, some hesitant bowing, or even the averting of eyes. Watching his entrance, and definitely not looking away, was Lady Dalrymple. 'Since he is here for such a short time,' she sniffed to a companion, 'it is as well we see so much of him.'

The 'King's Jaunt' was in part organised by Sir Walter Scott, and it ushered in something extraordinary, the start of the wholesale adoption of Highland iconography by many Scots. His first novel, the bestselling *Waverley*, was subtitled ''Tis Sixty Years Since', a reference to the time that had elapsed since Prince Charles and his Highland army had seized the city of Edinburgh. Its great success, and also the development of a romantic view of the Highlands and its people by the likes of James MacPherson, who claimed to have found ancient epic poetry that described a heroic past, probably persuaded Scott to clothe the visit, and the king, in tartan. It was a much preferable and very distinctive alternative to Presbyterian grey.

The bolts of tartan made into kilts and wraps were a version of a cultural cover-up. Only seventy years before George IV appeared at the Holyrood levee, the Highlanders and their lands had been the victims of repressive legislation that attempted – and succeeded – in breaking the power of the clans. Not only had there been a concerted campaign of genocide and clearance after Culloden, Acts of Parliament banning the wearing of tartan and the playing of the pipes were put in place and lasted until 1782. And yet here was a portly king swathed in the stuff, perhaps strathspeying, reeling and no doubt sweating around the halls of Holyrood Palace. Something had changed.

The political reality was that the Highlands and the clans had been neutralised, made safe and converted into a means to make Scotland look very different from England. Sir Walter Scott was a dedicated unionist, but he also strove to establish a different identity for those subjects who lived north of the border. And he managed to perpetrate an outrageous fiction, and not in his novels or poems. So that he could be presented as a new Jacobite king, Scott had persuaded George IV that through clear genealogical links he was as much a Stuart as Prince Charles had been, and that he would be even more popular in Scotland as a result. More, he was entitled to wear the Royal Tartan, what became known later as Royal Stuart, and so an order was placed for a large kilt and all the accessories with a London tailor, George Hunter & Co. It seems that the measurements, certainly according to Lady Dalrymple, were not quite right.

The King's Jaunt was the beginning of the adoption of Highland iconography by Lowlanders and the creation of a lucrative branch of the retail trade – the seemingly endless number of shops in the Royal Mile that sell tartan, kilts and rugs, and a completely spurious sense of the past.

34

Edinburgh's Disgrace

On 27 August 1822 the Duke of Hamilton led a procession from Parliament Square in the High Street to the top of Calton Hill. Followed by members of masonic lodges, no doubt wearing their embroidered aprons – for building of a sort was to begin that morning – and by royal commissioners as well as other assorted Edinburgh grandees, Hamilton walked for a little more than a mile before climbing the long steps up to Calton Hill's summit. The procession was timed to take place while George IV was in Edinburgh, but the king did not join it. At around twenty stone and plagued by varicose veins, he might have found the exertion too much. And what was about to happen certainly turned out to be too much for Edinburgh.

With the ceremonial help of the masonic lodges, and with all of the others no doubt decked out in formal finery, the Duke of Hamilton presided over the laying of the foundation stone of the National Monument of Scotland. It was intended to serve as a fitting war memorial to all of the Scottish soldiers and sailors (1,156 Scottish sailors and five naval captains out of twenty-seven died at Trafalgar) who had died in the Napoleonic Wars. The structure was to be modelled on the Parthenon on the Acropolis in Athens, and the leading advocate of the proposed design was Thomas Bruce, the 7th Earl of Elgin. It was another moment of convoluted irony.

In the summer of 1801 – the earl claiming that he had reached agreement with the Sublime Porte, the government of the Ottoman Empire in Istanbul – Elgin's representatives took a great deal of original ancient sculpture from the Parthenon frieze, a caryatid from the Erechtheion and a good many other very beautiful and precious objects. The removal of all this sculpture and its eventual transfer to Britain cost a great deal of money, and in 1816 the British government paid the Turks £35,000 in compensation. The Elgin Marbles, as they are now known, are on display in the British Museum, despite the Greek government's repeated calls for their return.

Edinburgh's Parthenon would not display legendary Greek warriors or centaurs but sculptures of Scottish heroes. Here is an extract from a contemporary memorandum:

> . . . to adopt the Temple of Minerva or the Parthenon of Athens, as the model of the monument, and to restore to the civilized [i.e. not the Turkish/Muslim] world that celebrated and justly admired edifice, without any deviation whatever, excepting the adaptation of the sculpture to the events and achievements of the Scottish heroes, whose prowess and glory it is intended to perpetuate . . .

Under the monument, catacombs were to be excavated in order to supply burial places for eminent Scots. It was designed, as one commentator noted, as a Scottish Valhalla, thereby mixing classical with Norse allusions.

In July 1822 the Royal Association of Contributors to the National Monument of Scotland was formed to raise the necessary funds. But despite the support of well-known Edinburgh figures such as Sir Walter Scott, the association's efforts appeared to lack momentum. Nevertheless, real masons began work in 1826, and the front elevation of

Scotland's Parthenon was built to a design by William Henry Playfair. And that was when it began, and when it ended. The association had raised only £16,000 of the £43,000 needed, and the monument was abandoned, unfinished, in 1829.

Various nicknames were coined for what became one of Edinburgh's most prominent landmarks: Edinburgh's Disgrace, Scotland's Folly, The Pride and Poverty of Scotland or Edinburgh's Folly. But it was just as well that the project failed. Fakes, or copies of buildings 'without any deviation whatever' from another era and another culture, should have no place in a city already blessed with unique, original architectural glories.

35

Edinburgh Medics

Most doctors in eighteenth- and nineteenth-century Edinburgh believed that the dead could be of great help to the living. In the development of the science of anatomy, central to an understanding of all branches of medicine, the dissection of human cadavers was an essential means of not only advancing knowledge but also of teaching student doctors. The problem was that there were too few dead bodies to meet increasing demand. In Scots law it was only the corpses of hanged criminals, suicides or orphaned children that could be used. This dearth gave rise to a grisly business. 'Resurrection men' prowled around graveyards, usually at night, looking for freshly filled lairs. They exhumed the bodies, transported them to Edinburgh and sold them, often for high prices, to those who taught medicine. Not all were associated with the university directly, and some set themselves up as private tutors in the streets around Old College.

One such anatomist was Dr Robert Knox. Apparently a gifted teacher, his lectures attracted hundreds of paying students, and when a cadaver was available for dissection, his classroom was crammed. Knox bought some of his bodies from two Irishmen, William Burke and William Hare, who had both worked as navvies on the Caledonian Canal connecting Glasgow with Edinburgh. Graveyards had become well guarded, overlooked by manned watchtowers (many of which survive), or fresh graves were locked in iron cages known as mortsafes. And so Burke and Hare simplified and speeded up the process. They began to murder people. Usually they suffocated them so as not to damage any organs and then sold the fresh bodies to Knox's assistants (who must have suspected something was amiss but said nothing). In 1828, over a period of ten months, Burke and Hare supplied sixteen cadavers for dissection.

When their crimes were discovered and both men arrested, William Hare turned King's evidence and, in return for immunity, testified against Burke. When the identity of their customer came to light, the Edinburgh mob took against Dr Knox (who was not charged) and the anatomist was forced to flee the city. As the judge put on his black cap to pronounce sentence, he no doubt took some satisfaction in telling Burke that after he had been hanged his body would be given up for dissection.

The notorious story of Burke and Hare is perhaps the best known to be associated with the Edinburgh Medical School. And that is a pity, for its history of advances in an understanding of the human body and developing all manner of treatments is one of glittering achievements since 1726. The Medical School is associated with no fewer than thirteen Nobel Prize laureates and its graduates have founded medical schools or universities all over the world, including five of the USA's seven Ivy League universities.

For its first century and a quarter, the school was led by a dynasty of three successive Alexander Monros. They linked theoretical training with the first teaching hospital in Britain, the Edinburgh Infirmary for the Sick Poor, located, of course, in Infirmary Street. It opened in 1730. The first Alexander Monro was supported by Edinburgh's progressive lord provost, George Drummond, who wanted to see the city become a centre of excellence in medicine. In 1738 work began on a larger building in Infirmary Street. It had 228 beds and a surgical operation theatre with 200 seats for students. It was the reason why these rooms were called operating theatres; there had to be room for an audience. Eventually the much larger Royal Infirmary was built in the 1880s in Lauriston Place, opposite George Heriot's, and it has only recently been replaced with a modern hospital on the outskirts of the city at Little France.

A succession of brilliant teachers ensured that the Edinburgh Medical School was rated as the best in the world, a reputation it retained until the First World War. Innovation accompanied excellent tuition, and perhaps one of the greatest doctors to practise in Edinburgh was James Simpson. At the age of twenty-eight he became Professor of Medicine and Midwifery in 1839. He introduced the use of anaesthesia in the process of childbirth, greatly easing labour pains, and he also designed obstetric forceps to gently pull babies out into the world. Simpson and his friends experimented on themselves. To find the most effective form of chloroform, they inhaled it. With one sample, they at first felt very cheerful and then all collapsed only to wake the following morning. That was the one, they agreed. James Simpson's contribution was remembered with the establishment of the Simpson Memorial Maternity Pavilion. Generations of babies were born in its sympathetic and warm atmosphere, given a wonderful start in the world.

In 1869 Sophia Jex-Blake was permitted to attend certain classes in the School of Medicine. It was a breakthrough but only a gradual process followed. It took twenty years for women to be accepted as medical undergraduates. In 1889 Elsie Inglis and her father opened the Edinburgh College of Medicine for Women. She was a gifted, dedicated doctor and an active suffragette. Inglis died in 1917 after a punishing period of service in Serbia in the First World War, treating casualties, many of whom had suffered terrible injuries. Truly loved and greatly missed, her body lay in state at St Giles, and when it was taken for burial in the Dean Cemetery, Edinburgh's streets were lined with mourners.

Elsie Inglis' memorial was a small but very different maternity hospital close to Holyrood Park. It opened in 1925, and it was a remarkable place, somewhere mothers could feel safe, knowing that expert help was on hand. Fathers were not excluded to pace the corridors but encouraged to take an active part in the birthing of their children, and the hospital was the scene of thousands of life-enhancing experiences. It was nothing less than a tragedy that the little hospital closed in 1988. It was perhaps one of the greatest monuments to Edinburgh's glittering medical traditions.

36

Expanding Edinburgh

During the nineteenth century the Old Town stagnated. The great tenements off the High Street degenerated into slums, some were unsafe, and, at the north-eastern corner of North Bridge, one collapsed in 1861, killing thirty-five tenants. It became known as Heave Awa Hoose after a young lad was found alive but buried in the rubble. As the rescuers scrabbled to find survivors, Joseph McIvor is said to have shouted, 'Heave awa, lads! I'm no' dead yet.' On the site, the building which became that most Edinburgh of institutions, Patrick Thomson's department store, was built. PTs was one of many such shops set up in the late nineteenth century: R. W. Forsyth and Jenners may have been the most upmarket and famous, but many generations of children were dragged around the January sales at Forsyth's, Binns, J. & R. Allan's and several other emporia such as Goldberg's in Tollcross. Most have disappeared. Perhaps John Lewis is the sole survivor.

As the New Town crept up and over Bearford's Parks, down the old Gabriel Road and across the Moray Estate, and the Old Town crumbled, other housing developments pitched between these extremes found a market amongst the middling sort of people. Those who could not afford the Georgian grandeur in the north but were anxious to escape the vermin, the stink and the damp closes of the High Street began to look to the south. Across the old Burgh Loch, which opened as a public park in 1860, new, modern, spacious tenements began to rise.

Sir George Warrender of Lochend owned much of the old Burgh Muir and had built himself Bruntsfield House. It now forms the core of James Gillespie's School. In 1850 he decided to lease substantial parcels of land for housing. By 1869 plans had been drawn up and the plots were being pegged out. Warrender made two conditions: the streets had to be named after branches of his family and their estates (most of these have Berwickshire connections – Marchmont, Lauderdale, Thirlestane and others) and that no shops should sell alcohol. The latter stipulation did not last, but there are still very few pubs in the area.

It was a huge scheme, rivalling the New Town, and the tenement flats proved very popular. Plaques on some of the façades offer a clue as to how the business of development was managed. Builders and architects built piecemeal and speculatively – not entire streets but only a few plots at a time – and when the tenements had been completed, they then sold them and left their initials as a memorial to enterprise. For example ABC is the Argyle Building Company in Argyle Place, EC is Edward Calvert & Co. and so on.

Most of the suburb that became known as Marchmont, after the main thoroughfare, was completed by 1914. And elsewhere in the inner city extensive tenement development took place, particularly in Tollcross, Bruntsfield and on either side of the arterial roads towards Dalkeith and the Borders. Unlike London, Edinburgh splits more decisively into north and south rather than east and west. Princes Street is the frontier between New Town formality and Old Town and Southside sprawl. The residents of the Grange, Church Hill, Morningside and Merchiston and other upmarket enclaves might object but the divide is broadly accurate.

Gorgie and Dalry developed industrially as well as residentially, and in the west some of Edinburgh's characteristic products were manufactured. Sometimes reeled off as the Three Bs – beer, biscuits and books – the companies making these thrived in the later nineteenth century. What first encouraged factories and warehouses in the west of the city was the digging of the Forth and Clyde canal from 1818 to 1822, and then the approach of the railway from the same direction. Before 1940 Edinburgh boasted twenty independent brewers, and as late as the1980s the powerful aroma of malting barley blew over the city. But brewing in Edinburgh has seen a steep decline in the last thirty years. For many decades McVitie's and Crawford's baked excellent biscuits. And many famous publishers, printers and papermakers were sustained by the city's schools, colleges and university and the needs of the legal and medical trades. Some vestiges of each industry remain, but by the end of the twentieth century the service sector employed four out of every five people in Edinburgh as manufacturing declined.

From the late eighteenth century, Edinburgh's villages gradually became its suburbs. The first of these was recorded as early as the twelfth century when Broughton – derived from the Old English for 'the farm by the brook' – something like Brooktun, belonged to the canons of Holyrood Abbey. On the eastern edge of the first New Town, the village remained distinct for a long time; its toll booth was finally demolished in 1829. The sole echo of its medieval shape is the line of Broughton Street. Unlike the rectilinear layout of the Georgian development on either side, it wiggles cheerfully downhill to London Street and the beautiful Mansfield Traquair, a former church now used principally as a wedding venue.

Stockbridge was originally a milling village on the Water of Leith, and its name remembers it as the site of a timber bridge. When St Bernard's Well became popular and fashionable amongst the better-off as a source of health-giving mineral water – that is, water with minerals, principally iron, in it – the village began to expand. Much of the land was in the estate of Sir Henry Raeburn, one of Britain's greatest portrait painters, and street names remember that. Between 1861 and 1911, rows of compact little houses known as the Colonies were built in Stockbridge by the Edinburgh Cooperative Building Company, which was founded by the tradesmen who built these affordable houses for people like themselves. On eleven sites all over the city, these beautifully designed little houses were often owned by their occupants in an era before mortgages.

Morningside was probably a fanciful, invented name, meaning something like Sunnyside, coined by a landowner in the area in the late seventeenth century. As a supposedly genteel suburb, its fanciness has become the butt of many jokes, not least about the place, metaphorically, having a 'fur coat but nae knickers'. A map of 1812 shows house building not only on either side of what became Morningside Road but also extending into the fields and parks behind the street line.

Colinton may have a claim to be the oldest village to become a suburb. In a red sandstone gorge carved out by the Water of Leith, its church was rededicated to St Cuthbert (something that often implies antiquity) by King Malcolm III in 1095, perhaps prompted by his wife, Queen Margaret. Like Stockbridge, it was a mill village, and Spylaw Mill was one of the first paper mills to supply Edinburgh's growing publishing output. Colinton House eventually became the fee-paying, boarding Merchiston Castle School.

The place name of Corstorphine is unusual and it has spawned some fanciful derivations. But it is a reference to the fact that the land was boggy and patterned with small lochs. It means 'Thorfinn's Crossing', a place where it was possible to walk through the area dry-shod. The village grew up around a castle and a fifteenth-century church, and into the modern period it remained fairly rural, escaping much of the industrialisation that overtook western Edinburgh. Corstorphine was only absorbed into the city in the middle of the twentieth century.

Subsequent development, especially in the twentieth century, has blurred the boundaries of these and other villages, but their identities remain distinct.

37

The Great Disruption

God, or more precisely, an interpretation of God's will, was about to send more spires soaring into the Edinburgh skyline and give the impression of an extremely devout community. In the early nineteenth century the Church of Scotland had been riven by ferocious faction-fighting over the issue of patronage. Who had the right to choose a new minister for the parish? Was it the congregation and its elders, or was it the laird or the superior? By 1843 matters had boiled into a confrontation, and at the General Assembly held in St Andrew and St George's Church in George Street, they boiled over. The Great Disruption of the Church of Scotland began with a dramatic walkout by those ministers who believed that congregations and their elders ought to take precedence over the preferences of the lairds. That bold decision left almost all of them without churches, church halls or manses, and a widespread building programme immediately began all over Edinburgh and the rest of Scotland. Perhaps its most obvious result can be seen at Holy Corner, at the foot of Church Hill, where four churches of the reformed faith face each other over the crossroads. A city of many spires and bell towers quickly grew up.

The seeds of the Disruption had been sown long before with the passing of the Patronage Act in 1712 which handed land-owners the power to appoint parish ministers without reference to the Kirk Session. This was a fundamental break with the precepts of the Reformation and the freedoms so dearly won in the Wars of the Covenant. A number of congregations, some of them in Edinburgh, refused to accept this, and they formed the Secession Kirk. It was the first of many fractures.

The General Assembly held in Edinburgh in 1843 was the culmination of a bitter conflict, and an extraordinary set-piece, a showdown. On one side stood the Moderates, who sought to avoid confrontation with the state, and on the other were the Evangelicals who asserted the right of kirk sessions to choose a new parish minister when vacancies occurred. For the first time, the Evangelicals were in a majority in the General Assembly.

The moment of schism came when the outgoing moderator, the Reverend Dr David Welsh, read out a statement of protest on 18 May. And then in a moment of high drama, he walked out of St Andrew and St George's Church followed by 121 ministers and 73 elders who rose from their seats to join him. Watched by huge crowds, the seceders made their way down Dundas Street to the Tanfield Hall in Canonmills. There, the first Disruption General Assembly was held with the charismatic Thomas Chalmers as moderator. In all, 473 ministers out of a total of 1,200 eventually left the established church to form the Free Church of Scotland, fewer than Chalmers hoped for and more than the Kirk feared. It was a turning moment in Scotland's history, played out in the streets of Edinburgh.

Perhaps the most spectacular, certainly the most widely visible consequence of the Great Disruption dominates the view of the Old Town from the north. The Assembly Hall towers darkly over Princes Street and the New Town from its vantage point near the top of the Mound, and in its forecourt there stands a statue of the pioneer reformer, John Knox. When the General Assembly of the Church of Scotland meets in May, the ministers and elders have to file past his stern gaze and remember their shared past.

38

Edinburgh Photographed

Watching the events of 18 May 1843 from the balcony of St Andrew and St George's Church was an observant young man. David Octavius Hill had made excellent drawings of the Great Fire of Edinburgh in the High Street and he was determined to make a good visual record of an equally seismic event in the life of Edinburgh and Scotland. With his business partner, Robert Adamson, he decided to record the events of the day in a completely new way.

Photography had been pioneered in England by William Henry Fox Talbot, who had developed the calotype process, a new way of making photographic paper by coating it with silver iodide. Very sensitive to light, the paper was inserted into a camera and then, once a subject had been posed and told to stay very still, it was exposed for one or two minutes if there was bright sunlight, longer if not. Hill had been trained as a painter, and his project was to create a vast group portrait of the General Assembly of 1843. Photography would help him greatly to do that. The problem was that drawing the necessary likenesses of each minister and elder was logistically impossible, since they were dispersed all over Scotland, and it would take far too long. So he and Adamson quickly shot calotypes of almost all who had been present and the vast, panoramic painting, measuring eleven feet by five feet, was finally completed more than twenty years later, in 1866. It was one of the largest group portraits ever made. And one of the last. The photographic techniques used like a sketchbook by Hill and Adamson would soon largely take the place of paintings of people.

Perhaps more importantly, Hill and Adamson ventured outside and shot calotypes of everyday scenes and everyday people, and these documentary records are the first to show what ordinary Scots looked like. Most attractive are the images made in the 1840s of the fishing community in Newhaven, west of Leith. There are both individual and group shots, and they have a quiet, everyday dignity, even confidence, as men, women and their children turn to the light and stay still so that the camera can capture their likeness.

One of the most atmospheric pictures is of a barefoot boy leaning on a creel dressed in an oversized pair of trousers rolled up to the knee and held by braces (his faither's auld breeks?). The image transcends charm as the lad stares intently off camera, keeping still, looking to a future that will much resemble his dad's past. There is a group shot of a dozen fishermen by an open-decked rowing boat, the sort they took out on the Forth fishing for herring. Known as the draves, shoals swam into the firth in huge numbers in the spring and summer, and that was a time of great activity both onshore and on the water. Many of the men wear the white trousers characteristic of the period, and in the picture all but one (who wears a toorie with a bobble at its crown) have put on their top hats, something kept for best and definitely not worn at work. Despite that small anomaly, these photographs are significant, the first series of images of ordinary people having their images, and their lives, recorded.

Each day, the fisherfolk, usually women, walked the three miles into Edinburgh to sell what they had caught. 'Caller herrin!' was what they shouted as they made their way up the

High Street – 'fresh herring'. It was a journey that only ceased in the 1960s. They may have passed close to Rock House at the western foot of Calton Hill. It was where Hill and Adamson set up their studio, and where many well-known people came to have their portrait taken. Hill's great skill in handling the camera was complemented by Adamson's feel for lighting and composition. But, sadly, their partnership was relatively short-lived. Over four years, they took more than 3,000 photographs, but by 1848 Robert Adamson was ill. He died that year, and David Octavius Hill seemed to lose heart, abandoning the studio after only a few months. He sold prints of the calotypes but returned to his career as a painter.

39

The Waverley

George IV's niece Queen Victoria became as besotted with Highland culture as he was – she even once remarked that 'in my heart, I am a Jacobite', even if she most certainly was not. She and Prince Albert began their love affair with Scotland in the 1840s, and by 1856 Holyrood Palace had been restored to more than its former glory. Once the Earl of Haddington had been restrained (by Act of Parliament) from quarrying the beautiful red stone from Salisbury Crags, the Queen's Park began to take shape. Using a little of the proceeds of his wildly successful novels, Sir Walter Scott had employed a group of destitute weavers from the west of Scotland (notorious for its radical politics) to build the wide path at the bottom of the crags now known as the Radical Road. And Prince Albert ordered the layout of carriage drives and the creation of Dunsapie Loch.

Much encouraged by royal patronage and the romance resonating from the worldwide success of the work of Scott, visitors began to make the long journey north to Scotland, and to Edinburgh in particular. A trickle grew into a flood when the railway arrived in 1846. Several lines met at the General Station at the east end of Princes Street Gardens. Very appropriately it quickly got the name Waverley after Scott's series of novels. Many of the people of Edinburgh, for some mysterious reason, attach the definite article and call it

'The Waverley'. Trinity Church was shifted southwards to make more room for platforms and the old Physic Garden moved much further north to the Royal Botanic Garden. At first, trains departed north and east through a tunnel dug under Princes Street, St Andrew Square, and emerging below Scotland Street. By 1862 another, more convenient route was excavated through Abbeyhill and the original tunnel closed up (it was used to store cars and other bulky goods until recently – and it still remains open, if very spooky). With twenty platforms, Edinburgh's principal railway station is one of the largest in Britain for passenger traffic. The great railway hotels at either end of Princes Street, the North British (now the Balmoral) and the Caledonian (now the Waldorf Astoria), meant that passengers and their luggage did not have far to travel (there was once a Princes Street Station behind the Caledonian). Cockburn Street was driven through the closes and the backlands off the High Street to allow access to the Waverley from the south.

Railways began to spread like veins all over nineteenth-century Edinburgh as different companies laid down tracks. One of the most significant was the Suburban Line, known as the 'Sub'. It eventually became a circular route from Waverley to the east, running to stations at Abbeyhill, Piershill, Portobello, Duddingston/Craigmillar, Newington, Blackford Hill, Morningside, Craiglockhart, Gorgie, Haymarket and back to the Waverley. This greatly stimulated the development of housing on the southern and eastern sides of the city as workers became commuters. The Sub rattled through the suburbs until passenger services ceased in 1962 as part of a national contraction of rail traffic. The line is still used by goods trains.

Competition was also a factor. Horse-drawn trams were running a circular route by 1872 from Marchmont to

Church Hill and then north to the West End of Princes Street. They often took more direct routes to the city centre, as did a developing bus service in the early twentieth century, and the suburban railways eventually fell silent. Trams had disappeared some years before when the electric service was discontinued in 1956.

But by the beginning of the twenty-first century, transport to and around Edinburgh had come full circle. After long deliberations and debate, the Waverley Railway (Scotland) Act became law in 2006 and preparations began to bring back trains to parts of suburban Edinburgh and also carry on the line down to the Borders. The line was eventually renamed the Borders Railway. One of the most persuasive aspects of the campaign to reinstate the line was the perceived need for a rail service for Edinburgh commuters coming from the south and east of the city, mostly from Midlothian. Councillors were anxious to keep as many cars as possible out of the already congested streets of the capital. Six suburban stations were opened at Brunstane, Newcraighall, Shawfair, Eskbank, Newtongrange and Gorebridge, and from the latter the line would then carry trains south to Stow, Galashiels and on to the terminus at Tweedbank. Passenger services began on 6 September 2015, and five days later the new railway was officially opened by Her Majesty Queen Elizabeth II on the day that she became Britain's longest reigning monarch.

The business case for the new line had estimated that in the first year of operation there would be 650,000 return journeys made between Waverley and Tweedbank and all the stations between. Some thought that unduly optimistic. But in fact the line turned out to be much more popular: in September 2016 it was revealed that more than a million passengers had used the Borders Railway, most of them Edinburgh commuters.

The economic impact of the new rail link was not difficult to measure. Immediately to the south of the city a house-building boom began. The number of new houses doubled year on year in Midlothian, and around Shawfair Station it is anticipated that 4,000 new houses will be built in the next twenty-five years as a small new town takes shape, one that will have a railway station as its transport nucleus.

In 2014 trams reappeared in the centre of Edinburgh when a line was opened at York Place that could take passengers out to Edinburgh Airport. In 2023 the line was extended to Newhaven, and it runs for eleven and a half miles in total. Both the coming of the railway and the trams have had the beneficial effect of removing many cars from the middle of the city and not only improving its air quality but also making the streets more friendly to pedestrians.

40

Edinburgh-on-Sea

Six coastal settlements lie to the north of Edinburgh and are now part of the city. Strung out in a line on the Forth shore, Joppa, Portobello, Leith, Newhaven and Granton are now all linked, but they retain distinct identities. Farthest west is the oldest of these communities, the village of Cramond. Archaeologists have discovered evidence of people living there since around 8500 BC.

Leith's name probably derives, like Edinburgh's, from Old Welsh. It certainly comes from the name of the little river, and river names are often the oldest in the landscape. It is said that it is cognate to *llaith*, simply meaning water, but that is not how it is listed in *Y Geiriadur Mawr*, the Great Dictionary of the Welsh language. Instead, it may be a reference to a muddy place, where the Water of Leith's outfall into the Forth was once more of a delta and not canalised and contained as it is now. In either case, 'Leith' speaks of an old settlement.

The place comes on written record in 1128 when it belonged to the canons of Holyrood Abbey and was seen as two distinct places: North Leith on one side of the river and South Leith on the other. That division has persisted. The king's burgh of Edinburgh retained controlling rights over the harbour because it was a vital trading link that produced revenue for the crown. After the seizure of Berwick in 1482 by England, Leith became and remained Scotland's most important port

until the development of the Clyde and Glasgow in the nineteenth century. At that time, in 1833, the town became
independent, designated a parliamentary burgh with its own
MP because the upkeep of the docks had almost bankrupted
Edinburgh. That independence lasted for almost a century. In
1920 a plebiscite was held on the proposed union with
Edinburgh, and even though 26,810 Leithers voted against it
and only 4,340 supported it, the necessary legislation was
forced through. The former Boundary Bar on Leith Walk (the
name changed in 2002) sat astride the old border between the
burghs, and it was said, and perhaps it is true, that because the
licensing laws in Leith were more liberal, drinkers could
simply move from one end of the bar to the other to continue
to enjoy their evening out for another half hour.

In 1996 what used to be known as the Scottish Office
moved from New St Andrew's House in the St James Centre
(and St Andrew's House below Calton Hill) in the middle of
Edinburgh to Victoria Quay in Leith. It was a signal for
revival, and the old port saw a great deal of new development
in housing and the opening of high-end hotels and restaurants. Leith has become fashionable as a direct consequence
of devolution and the establishment of a Scottish Parliament.
And so has Edinburgh, although its citizens will claim that it
was never out of fashion.

To the east of Leith lie two exotic and much younger place
names. Joppa comes on record in the *Statistical Account* of
1794 and it appears to be a version of Jaffa, the Israeli port on
the Mediterranean Sea. Quite why that choice was made is
obscure. Joppa began a much more mundane life as a mining
village housing those who worked at the coal heughs of Easter
Duddingston, near where the dual carriageway of the A1 now
begins. There were also salt pans on the shore, and these
almost certainly predated the name of Joppa, for salt was in

great demand to preserve the beef processed in the Cowgate and the fish caught in the Forth.

Now Joppa is a community of pleasant streets of well-set terraces and tidy tenements. As its name implies, Seaview Terrace has a splendid vista across to the Fife coast. On 16 October 1939 war came roaring over that idyllic horizon as the Luftwaffe mounted a daylight raid on three warships lying at anchor at Rosyth. As German planes were shot down by naval artillery, houses in Joppa were damaged. The bodies of Luftwaffe pilots were buried in the graveyard at St Philip's Church, now Joppa and Portobello Parish Church, the first enemy casualties to be interred in British soil.

Portobello was at first a consequence of naval action. On wild land known as Figgate Whins, between Leith and Musselburgh, a veteran of the British Navy's capture of Puerto Bello in Panama decided to build a house, and he named it after the action of 1739. The house is no more – Portobello Town Hall stands on its site – but the name lived on and attracted a cheerier meaning as the seaside town became a popular resort.

Portobello has a dual identity and significance – one being the town and resort, the other being the site of potteries which date to the 1760s and lasted for 200 years. They formed part of a nationally important pottery industry based around the Forth which rivalled the more famous Stoke-on-Trent potteries. Two early twentieth-century kilns survive (the two only such kilns in Scotland) as a visible reminder to this industry and its workers. In time the remains of the potteries' Georgian harbour may emerge from the sands if the conditions are right.

At low tide, Portobello Sands is wide, and Prince Charles Edward Stuart reviewed the Jacobite army there before they marched east to Prestonpans and a famous victory. In the nineteenth century military connotations faded as trains and trams brought day trippers and holidaymakers. The better-off in Edinburgh took to building summer residences at Portobello, and in 1833, the same time as Leith, the town was awarded burgh status. 'Porty' became Edinburgh's promenade as the idea of the seaside began to become attractive around Britain's coasts. In 1871 Portobello Pier was built to the design of Thomas Bouch. He was also the architect of the Tay Rail Bridge that was damaged badly by a storm and collapsed with considerable loss of life in 1879. The pier was demolished in 1917. Perhaps it was looking a little rickety.

Portobello saw its tourist business decline in the middle of the twentieth century, but recently revival has stirred. The promenade and the wide sands are popular once more, and at least a dozen excellent restaurants have opened, some selling street food and a few offering wonderful sea views and excellent menus. From nearby Musselburgh, the products of Di Rollo and Luca, two superb ice-cream makers, are available to complete the picture of being by the seaside.

More naval action was on the mind of one of Scotland's most ambitious, and foolhardy, kings when in 1506 James IV founded his royal dockyard at Newhaven, west of Leith. The old haven was at Blackness, between South Queensferry and Bo'ness, and it was too small. James wanted to build a huge battleship. Known as the *Great Michael*, after the Archangel Michael, it was vast at 240 feet in length and with a 10-foot-thick hull. For comparison, Christopher Columbus' *Santa Maria*, the largest of the ships to cross the Atlantic in 1492, was only fifty-eight feet in length. The ship needed 'all the woods of Fife' as well as a great deal of imported timber. It also needed skills not found in Scotland, and shipwrights from Flanders and Holland crossed the North Sea. There were twenty-four guns to deliver broadsides (one of them may have been Mons Meg, now found in Edinburgh Castle) and thirty-six pieces of smaller artillery. On board was a crew of 300 sailors, 120 gunners and 1,000 marines. The *Great Michael* was the greatest gunship built in Europe up to that time.

It was not intended for use against the English navy. James IV planned to sail his great ship into the Mediterranean at the head of a seaborne crusade to take back the Holy Land for Christianity. It never happened. And nor was it ever likely to happen. Instead, the Treaty of Perpetual Peace that followed the marriage of the king to Margaret Tudor turned out to redefine perpetual, and the *Great Michael* sailed south to attack English ships. It quickly became clear that the costs of the maintenance of this huge vessel were too much for the Scottish exchequer, so the *Great Michael* was sold to King Louis XII of France for the knockdown price of 40,000 livres. It ended its life rotting in the harbour at Brest in Britanny.

Long after the madcap ambitions of James IV had been forgotten, Newhaven's fishermen harvested oysters instead of building ships, and fishwives walked into Edinburgh carrying creels of them, calling out 'Caller ou!' – fresh oysters. At the end of the eighteenth century the herring began to come into the Forth, and the open rowing boats in Hill and Adamson's photographs went out after the draves. A close-knit community, Newhaveners claim descent from the Flemish and Dutch shipwrights who built the *Great Michael*, and they call themselves the Bow-Tows, an obscure reference, perhaps, to the Society of Free Fishermen founded at the end of the sixteenth century. There is now a monthly newsletter called *The Bow-Tow*. The name is said to have some vague link to a sense of being between land and sea. It seems more likely that it is connected to a different sort of link, the way in which fishermen moored their boats in the busy little harbour. There being little room, they were tied or towed only at the bow and not the stern and bow.

Between Newhaven and Cramond a vast Victorian harbour was built on Wardie Muir at the initiative of the Duke of Buccleuch in 1835, who owned land around Dalkeith and in Edinburgh. Hailed as 'a magnificent enterprise', it included a large hotel and offices in Granton Square and saw the construction of a pier completed in 1845. The *Statistical Account* of 1845 noted that 'upon the pier are 10 jetties, 2 low water slips, 11 warehouses and 19 cranes'. The stone for construction came from the bed of the Firth of Forth, from Granton sea quarry. By 1855 the western breakwater was complete and equipped with steam cranes and a slip for the construction and repair of ships up to 12,000 tonnes. The world's first railway ferry began to run from Granton to Burntisland in 1847, and it linked Edinburgh with lines to Perth and Dundee. The service was only discontinued when the Forth Bridge was finished in 1890. The West Harbour was enlarged to accommodate a trawler fleet in 1936. But after the Second World War, Granton's importance as a port began to decline, and its facilities became industrial archaeology. Container ships sailed on to Grangemouth, where unloading facilities were better, the decline and disappearance of Edinburgh's paper mills meant that imports of esparto grass were no longer needed; fishing became concentrated further north at Peterhead and Fraserburgh; and automation dispensed with the need for the small fleet that serviced lighthouses. Now Granton harbour is mostly an anchorage for yachts and other pleasure craft.

One of the purest survivals of a place name in Old Welsh, Cramond is from *Caer Amon*, 'the (Roman) Fort on the River'. The remains of the fort were excavated and identified first in 1954, but in 1997 a sensational new discovery was made. Robert Graham, who operated a ferry near the mouth of the Almond, spotted an object sticking out of the mud. It turned out to be a large sculpture of a lioness killing a bound male prisoner. She is sinking her teeth into his head. About five feet long, it was probably made for the tomb of a Roman military commander or some sort of dignitary. The Cramond Lioness was one of the most vivid and important Roman discoveries in Scotland for decades, and it is on permanent display in the National Museum of Scotland in Edinburgh.

Many centuries after the end of the Roman Empire, Cramond developed as an industrial village, and the riverside was the site of mills. In 1751 the Cramond Iron Works started production, and between 1770 and 1860 the Cadell company employed about a hundred workers in four mills along the riverbank, including the Fairafar Forge. The earliest commercially produced steel in Scotland was made in Cramond.

By the middle of the nineteenth century, with good transport links to the centre of the city, Cramond forgot its industrial past and became a highly desirable, leafy suburb that was separated from industrial Granton and fishy Newhaven by wide parkland and golf courses. The particular pronunciation of Cramond, with a flattened 'a' sometimes raises a smile. Muriel Spark's Miss Jean Brodie, not surprisingly, spent a good deal of her time in the village. Naval matters left a more modern and permanent mark. Cramond Island is linked to the shore by a causeway built during the Second World War to service a battery that could defend the upper Forth and Rosyth naval dockyard. Beside it runs a line of concrete pillars designed as a barrier to prevent hostile ships approaching closer to the shore.

There is an attractive promenade that begins (or ends) in Cramond, and it takes walkers eastwards to Granton and Newhaven, through Leith by various means, and on to Portobello and Joppa. It runs through a very different Edinburgh.

41

Elementary, Edinburgh

The world's most famous detective was born in Edinburgh. His creator, Arthur Conan Doyle, was also born in the city, at 11 Picardy Place at the top of Leith Walk, in 1859. Having attended boarding schools in England and Austria, he matriculated at the Edinburgh Medical School in 1876 and also studied botany at the Botanic Gardens. As a student, Conan Doyle seemed to be driven to write fiction, and his first academic article appeared to point the way to what made him one of the most popular authors of the age. 'Gelsemium as a Poison', published in the *British Medical Journal* in 1879, was a piece of original research thought to be useful in the investigation of murder. In 1881 Conan Doyle graduated from Edinburgh as Bachelor of Medicine and Master of Surgery, but then went on to a higher qualification as an MD or Doctor of Medicine. His dissertation, once again, involved the study of a fatal disease, neurosyphilis.

After graduation, Arthur Conan Doyle set up in general practice in Plymouth and later moved to Southsea. It turned out to be difficult to attract patients, and so during gaps between appointments the doctor continued to write, but with mixed success. Then inspiration, or perhaps frustration, struck. Conan Doyle remembered his medical training, the art of diagnosis, and also the effects of poison and how to deduce that it had been used. In three weeks he wrote his first novel, *A Study in Scarlet*, and it featured Sherlock Holmes and his friend, Dr John Watson. As a 'consulting detective', Holmes solves a series of murders that are baffling the police and some of which involved the use of poison. The novel was sold to Ward, Lock & Co. and published in 1886. It was followed by three more full-length novels and fifty-six short stories. Holmes and Watson became a literary phenomenon, and an early catchphrase went into the language. Whenever Watson was surprised, even astonished at Holmes' abilities at deduction, and asked how he could possibly know who had murdered whom and why, the great detective would reply, 'Elementary, my dear Watson.'

Conan Doyle knew precisely where the model for his great creation had come from, and it was not his imagination. He had met Dr Joseph Bell, a surgeon and lecturer in the Edinburgh Medical School, and become his clerk at the Royal Infirmary in 1877. When Bell gave lectures to medical students, he laid great emphasis on the observation of patients. In order to arrive at the correct diagnosis, it was vital to look closely as well as listen to what people said about what ailed them. Students were as wide-eyed as Dr Watson when Bell picked out a stranger and by observation deduced what his job was and indeed what he had been doing recently and where he had been while doing it.

Dr Bell was a pioneer in forensic science, the application of scientific methods in legal and criminal investigations, and also in forensic pathology in attempts to establish the cause of death. These are expertises shared with Sherlock Holmes, who also made a habit of observing everyone he met in the course of an investigation. There was also a relentless application of logic. In 'The Adventure of Silver Blaze', about the theft of a horse, Holmes wonders why the dog in the stable yard did not bark when the animal was stolen. And it is that curious fact that eventually leads Holmes to solve the case. Like 'Elementary, my dear Watson', 'the dog that didn't bark' is also a phrase that has entered the language.

Arthur Conan Doyle wrote to Joseph Bell in 1892: 'It is most certainly to you I owe Sherlock Holmes . . . round the centre of deduction and inference and observation which I have heard you inculcate I have tried to build up a man.' It may be that the character of Holmes owed even more to the Edinburgh surgeon. In 1874, his wife Edith died at the early age of thirty-four, and Bell also outlived their son, Benjamin. The image of a solitary man single-mindedly devoted to his work is reinforced by photographs. There seems to be a close similarity between drawings of Holmes (from Conan Doyle's descriptions of him) and the hollow-cheeked, unsmiling surgeon. There is even a photograph of Bell wearing an Inverness cape, but with a cap and not a deerstalker hat.

When Conan Doyle wrote *A Study in Scarlet*, he was living in Southsea. Although he had no doubt visited London, he cannot have known the city well. More than one academic admirer of the Holmes stories believes that Conan Doyle relied on his memories of Edinburgh to create Baker Street and its environs and cloak them all in pea-soupers.

Such was the success of the tales of the great detective and his companion that their creator tired of them and began to consider ending the series. He wrote to his mother: 'I think of slaying Holmes . . . and winding him up for good and all. He takes my mind from better things.' Mrs Conan Doyle was appalled: 'You won't! You can't! You mustn't!' Instead, the author demanded larger and larger royalties from publishers in order to discourage them. But it didn't work. They agreed to all he asked, he became one of the highest-paid writers of the age, and the appetite for Holmes stories remained undimmed. But eventually it all became too much, and in the story, 'The Final Problem', it really was final as the great detective plunged to his death over the Reichenbach Falls. Or did he? Such was the public outcry that Holmes and Watson reappeared in perhaps the best and most gripping of all the stories, *The Hound of the Baskervilles.*

Edinburgh remembers Sherlock Holmes with a statue of him in the centre of Picardy Place, where his creator was born. Complete with Inverness cape, ruffled a little by the wind blowing up Leith Walk, wearing a deerstalker hat and holding a curly calabash pipe, the great detective looks pensive, as though he is mulling over the evidence in a particularly thorny case. And he also looks very like Dr Joseph Bell, something that would have pleased Arthur Conan Doyle.

42

Precipitous City

Robert Louis Stevenson wrote to Arthur Conan Doyle in 1886: 'My compliments on your very ingenious and very interesting adventures of Sherlock Holmes . . . can this be my old friend, Joe Bell?' A little older than Conan Doyle, Stevenson was born in 1850 in Edinburgh, the son of a leading designer and builder of some of Scotland's most spectacular lighthouses. The boy spent many summers at his grandfather's house in Colinton, and the fresh country air, away from the smoke of the city, was thought to help his weak chest and troubled breathing. When Stevenson was six years old, the family moved to Heriot Row in the New Town, and his memory of the long winter evenings, looking out of his bedroom window, appeared in 'The Lamplighter', an atmospheric memory of the Victorian city. Here are the final four lines:

For we are very lucky, with a lamp before the door,
And Leerie stops to light it as he lights so many more;
And O! before you hurry by with ladder and with light,
O Leerie, see a little child and nod to him tonight.

In 1886, the same year as *A Study in Scarlet* came out, *Kidnapped* was published. Robert Louis Stevenson advertised it as a 'boys' novel' and it appeared in serial form in the magazine *Young Folks*. But in fact it was one of the greatest works of historical fiction since Sir Walter Scott laid down his pen. Opening with David Balfour's encounter with his uncle – or was he? – Ebenezer with his blunderbuss at the House of Shaws, beckoning for him to come upstairs, where several were missing, invisible in the darkness, it becomes a riveting, page-turning chase across the Highlands, set in 1751. Also in 1886, *The Strange Case of Dr Jekyll and Mr Hyde* was published, and that decade saw a golden period from Stevenson with *The Black Arrow*, *The Master of Ballantrae*, *The Wrong Box* and the delightful, gentle *A Child's Garden of Verses*, which included 'The Lamplighter'. *Treasure Island*, perhaps his most famous work, had been published in 1883.

For much of the twentieth century, Robert Louis Stevenson was regarded simply as a children's author. That is utter nonsense. His clear language and precise, spare style are entirely at the service of brilliant storytelling, and not only to suit a younger readership. He wrote several very great novels that are accessible to both adults and children and introduced them to reading, and kept them reading.

Stevenson's ill health drove him away from damp and foggy Edinburgh, first south to Bournemouth and then finally to the Pacific island of Samoa where he was given the native name of Tusitala, the Teller of Tales. After completing *Catriona*, a sequel to *Kidnapped*, and two other novels, he became depressed, fearing that his powers were fading and that his health might decline so much that he would become a useless invalid. 'I wish to die in my boots,' he wrote, 'no more Land of Counterpane for me. To be drowned, to be shot, to be thrown from a horse – ay, to be hanged, rather than pass again through that slow dissolution.'

Sometime after that bout of depression, Stevenson began writing again, a novel called *Weir of Hermiston*, one that he would not complete. 'It is so good that it frightens me.' But then, when making mayonnaise with his wife Fanny, Stevenson felt something happen. He was having a stroke, a cerebral haemorrhage, and a few hours later, one of Scotland's very greatest writers was dead. He was only forty-four years old.

Knowing for many years that he was ill and that his life was likely to be short, Stevenson had written a requiem for his headstone:

> Under the wide and starry sky,
> Dig the grave and let me lie.
> Glad did I live and gladly die,
> And I laid me down with a will.
> This be the verse you grave for me:
> Here he lies where he longed to be;
> Home is the sailor, home from the sea,
> And the hunter home from the hill.

In all his travels, Robert Louis Stevenson never forgot Edinburgh and how it formed him. Six months before he died, he wrote to his friend, the novelist S.R. Crockett: 'I shall never see Auld Reekie. I shall never set my foot again upon the heather. Here I am until I die, and here I will be buried.' After his death, Fanny found a poem in the unfinished manuscript of *Weir of Hermiston*. It is heart-breakingly beautiful, an elegy from exile, five lines that capture Edinburgh in the late nineteenth century, but that are also timeless:

> I saw rain falling and the rainbow drawn
> On Lammermuir. Hearkening I heard again
> In my precipitous city beaten bells
> Winnow the keen sea wind. And here afar,
> Intent on my own race and place I wrote.

43

Round and Oval Balls

Like Waverley Station, Edinburgh's oldest professional football team was named after a novel by Sir Walter Scott. Heart of Midlothian FC was founded in 1874, and the team badge is a version of the mosaic of cobblestones in the High Street, not far from St Giles. At first the club played its matches in the East Meadows, just to the south of George Square, and at Powderhall. In 1886 they moved to Tynecastle, which the club leased from Edinburgh Corporation. Despite several recently mooted moves to sites on the edge of the city that might have had space for car and coach parking, Hearts, as they are known (or the Jam Tarts or Jambos, a reference to their maroon jerseys), have remained at the Tynecastle stadium near the centre of Edinburgh. Now fully seated, as opposed to terracing where the crowds stood to watch the matches, the ground has a capacity of almost 21,000.

A year after Heart of Midlothian was formed, Hibernian Football Club came into existence. It was originally the preserve of the Irish Catholic community centred on the Cowgate; its name is the Latin version of Ireland and its green shirts a further reference to the Emerald Isle. In 1892 the club leased Easter Road, their current home, and matches began to be played there a year later. Hibs were the first team from the east of Scotland to win the Scottish Cup when they defeated Dumbarton 2–1 in the final in Glasgow in 1887. Six years later, the ban on Protestant players was lifted, and gradually support for both Hearts and Hibs became a matter of geography rather than religion. Fans of the latter tended to come from northern and eastern Edinburgh while Hearts' support was generally in the west of the city.

In the First World War, many Hearts players enlisted and formed part of McCrae's Battalion. Their bravery and sacrifice are remembered in the splendid clock erected as a memorial at Haymarket.

Perhaps Hibernian's most successful era was between 1939 and 1954, when their forward line (Gordon Smith, Eddie Turnbull, Willie Ormond, Lawrie Reilly and Bobby Johnstone) was known as the Famous Five. Each one scored more than a hundred goals for the club as they won the Scottish League in 1950–51 by ten points, in the following season by four points and only narrowly failed to make it three in a row in the season after that. All of the Famous Five played for Scotland, and a stand at Easter Road is named after them.

In what was a golden era for Edinburgh football Heart of Midlothian had a long run of success after Hibs had been so consistent. Between 1954 and 1962 the club won two league titles, one Scottish Cup and four Scottish League Cups. Their forward line of Jimmy Wardhaugh, Alfie Conn and Willie Bauld (known as the Terrible Trio) was also formidable, and at wing-half, what might now be called midfielders, were two more outstanding players in Dave Mackay and John Cumming. The latter was the only player of that era to win all seven medals for Hearts' singular run of excellent results.

In 1871 the first ever rugby union international was played in Edinburgh at Raeburn Place in Stockbridge. In a twenty-a-side match played in two halves of fifty minutes each, Scotland defeated England. Thirteen years earlier, the city saw another first. The oldest continuous club rugby fixture was first played in Edinburgh in 1858 between Merchiston Castle School and the former pupils of Edinburgh Academy. When the Scottish Rugby Union was founded in 1873, four Edinburgh clubs joined three from Glasgow and St Andrews University. Merchistonians, Edinburgh Academicals, Edinburgh University and the Royal High School Former Pupils can claim to be amongst the oldest clubs in the city, and in Britain.

At first the Scottish Rugby Union was known as the Scottish Football Union, and confusion was only cured in 1924 when the name was at last changed. International matches had been moved from Raeburn Place in 1893 to Inverleith Park when the ground was purchased by the SFU. The first match to be played there was a 9–3 defeat by Ireland. One of Scotland's greatest and most loved athletes was also a gifted rugby player. In 1922 and 1923 Eric Liddell played on the wing for Scotland and his speed took away from defences as he scored tries.

Both football and rugby became very popular, in part because of changes in working patterns that saw many men have Saturday afternoons off, and it was decided that after the First World War, a new and larger stadium for rugby internationals was needed. A nineteen-acre plot in the west of the city was bought from the Edinburgh Polo Club. On 21 March 1925 England was the first visiting team to play at Murrayfield, and in a very satisfactory baptism for the new ground, Scotland defeated England to win a first Five Nations Championship Grand Slam. But it was not the prelude to any sort of golden era. The national team would have to wait until 1984 to win another one.

Perhaps Edinburgh and Britain's greatest athlete was born and raised near Murrayfield. Chris Hoy won no fewer than six Olympic gold medals in cycling and an extraordinary eleven world championships. He remains the second most successful Olympian of all time.

44

War City

A century ago, a fitting memorial to the sacrifice and the terrible slaughter of the First World War was planned. Scotland's National War Memorial would stand on the rocky heights in the centre of Edinburgh Castle and along its walls those regiments who had all suffered huge losses – almost 150,000 Scots died in the long years of attritional warfare in the trenches in Flanders – would be remembered. The names of every one of the fallen would be recorded, the regimental standards would hang there, and countless stories of courage and hardihood would be told. The project was the brainchild of the 8th Duke of Atholl, John Stewart-Murray, himself a soldier who had served in the First World War. He felt strongly that Scotland should have its own memorial, separate and distinct from England's, or indeed the nation's memorial, the Cenotaph in London. It should be 'truly Scottish, carried out by Scottish money, Scottish brains, and Scottish hands'.

Sadly, the whole enterprise was dogged by controversy and mean-spiritedness. Few seemed happy with Sir Robert Lorimer's neo-Gothic design. Apparently, it looked to some like 'a huge jelly mould'. Others thought Glasgow should be its location. A reasonably modest sum of £150,000 was needed but, by 1920, only £53,000 had been raised, and the memorial was only made possible by a huge donation from Alexander Lyle, the sugar magnate.

In truth, Edinburgh Castle was indeed the most appropriate location. It is Scotland's most famous military landmark, and it rises above the nation's capital city. The castle was also heavily involved in the First World War, serving as a recruitment centre, a training base, a prison and a military hospital. It was the regimental headquarters of the Royal Scots, sometimes referred to as Edinburgh's regiment, and the oldest foot regiment in the British Army. It recruited more than 100,000 men to fight in the First World War, won six Victoria Crosses, but lost nearly 11,000 men in the brutal battles in Flanders and elsewhere.

Not all of the wounds inflicted in the trenches were physical. A former hotel in south-west Edinburgh, Craiglockhart House, was set up as a hospital specifically to deal with shell shock, what is now called PTSD, post-traumatic stress disorder. This was the general term for extreme reactions to the intensity of the thunderous, repeated bombardments and the fighting. Soldiers suffering from shell-shock often felt helpless, panicked, sometimes fled and sometimes could not sleep or even walk and talk. After the Battle of the Somme in 1916, the number of sufferers increased enormously.

Two of Craiglockhart's most famous patients were the war poet, Wilfred Owen, and the poet and writer, Siegfried Sassoon. In a letter sent in 1917, Sassoon called the hospital 'Dottyville'. Owen's 'Anthem for Doomed Youth' was written at Craiglockhart in the same year and it became emblematic of the waste of human life in the trenches. The title was suggested by Sassoon, and he also made some amendments to the verses. A manuscript copy of the great poem survives with both men's handwriting on it. Despite his shell shock and his views on the futility of the war so eloquently expressed in the great lyric, Wilfred Owen returned to France in August 1918 and was awarded the Military Cross for bravery. Tragically, he was killed in action on 4 November, only a week before the armistice.

On the night of 2 April 1916, two Zeppelins, German airships, dropped bombs on Leith and the Grassmarket. The police had received a warning of the raid, or at least the approach of the aircraft, probably contacted when they were seen flying over the North Sea coast, one making landfall at St Abbs, the other at Newcastle. The raid was in fact aimed at the naval dockyard at Rosyth, but poor visibility persuaded the pilots to drop their bombs first on Leith and then, following the Water of Leith in the fading light, on the city. Premises around Leith Docks were damaged, a whisky bond making a great conflagration, and two people were killed. More bombs fell in the Grassmarket and close to Edinburgh Castle, and the White Hart Hotel and the County Hotel in Lothian Road were badly hit. In Newington seven people lost their lives, five of them as a result of a direct hit on a house in Marshall Street. During the raid, thirteen people died in Leith and Edinburgh, and a further twenty-four were badly injured. The Zeppelins brought more than death and destruction; they brought the appalling realities of war directly into civilian lives. And the raid may have influenced the design of the interior of the Scottish National War Memorial in Edinburgh Castle.

Sir Robert Lorimer had brought together 200 stonemasons, builders, designers, artists and craftsmen to create a remarkable monument. When it was opened in 1927 by King George V and Queen Mary, the interior was much commented on. Around the walls was a beautiful frieze of bronze figures designed by Alice Meredith Williams. Her husband, Morris, an art teacher at Fettes College, had fought in the war, and Alice made much use of his drawings. Unusually, the frieze shows all ranks of servicemen and women, and even animals. The chief executive of the memorial, Susan Flintoff, said:

'Every single service and rank is represented in the frieze . . . army, navy, air force, the women's services, medics, horses. There's even a camel, a pigeon, donkeys and dogs.'

Since it opened in 1927, the monument has recorded the name of every Scottish soldier to die in action, from the Second World War to Iraq and Afghanistan. It is a beautiful, surprising and deeply affecting place, a fitting monument.

45

Ugly Edinburgh

By the time the Nazis came to power in 1933, they had identified scapegoats for many of Germany's ills after defeat in the First World War. Amongst others, the Jews were blamed and persecuted. A similar reaction against the economic woes of the 1920s and 1930s, the Great Depression and the widespread unemployment of those years – although with very much less appalling consequences – wormed its way into Scottish politics. By 1929, the Church of Scotland had healed the rifts of the Disruption and reunited with the United Free Church, bringing together 90 per cent of Scotland's Presbyterians. But the Kirk was sometimes very reactionary in its views and it was especially angry at the provision made for Catholic schooling in the 1918 Education Act (Scotland). Shocking racist language issued from pulpits and pamphlets as the national church talked of 'inferior people' and 'an alien race'. In 1923 a pamphlet entitled 'The Menace of the Irish Race to our Scottish Nationality' was widely circulated. Demonised as drunken, promiscuous ('breeding like rabbits'), uncivilised and the carriers of deadly disease (typhus was popularly known as 'Irish Fever'), the Catholic Irish living in Scotland became the focus of political spite, and worse.

One of the worst excesses broke out in the summer of 1935 in, of all places, the douce and leafy Edinburgh suburb of Morningside. Violently anti-Catholic and against further

Irish immigration, the Protestant Action Society was founded in 1930 by John Cormack, and he and several others were elected as councillors to Edinburgh Corporation, gaining 31 per cent of the vote, more than the Labour candidates.

The first Eucharistic Conference, the first major event of Catholic worship to be staged in Scotland since the Reformation, had been organised, and it centred on St Peter's Church in Morningside and St Benet's, the nearby residence of the Archbishop of St Andrews and Edinburgh. As the date, 25 June, approached, the atmosphere in the city began to darken and rumours were spreading of a violent Protestant reaction. The conference would attract Catholics from all over Scotland, and the archbishop, Andrew MacDonald, was very concerned for their safety, and with good reason. Here is an extract from his letter to *The Scotsman*:

The office which I have the honour to hold has been the object of gross insult and of the vilest accusations. For some time it has hardly been possible for a priest to appear in the city without being subjected to unspeakable indignities. They have been not only the target for vile abuse and most filthy and obscene language, but they have repeatedly been spat upon and molested in public streets. In the factories and public works Catholic employees, and particularly defenceless girls, have suffered bitter persecution, as contemptible as it is cowardly, and strenuous efforts have been made to induce employers to dismiss Catholics on the grounds of their religion alone.

On the evening of the conference, the rumours turned out not to be exaggerated. Crammed into trams arriving from all over the city, encouraged by the ranting prejudices of John Cormack and others, more than 10,000 supporters of

Protestant Action flooded the streets of Morningside. The police had set up a cordon around the outdoor service, and the rioters made repeated attempts to charge through. When worshippers attempted to leave, their buses were pelted with stones, and, ironically, at a Morningside crossroads known as Holy Corner (there are three churches in close proximity), a bus full of terrified men, women and children was stopped and overturned. Mounted police charged the mob and managed to disperse them. Jim Marin remembered: 'I was chased along Canaan Lane by a group of gentlemen when I was just seven years old because I was dressed in the uniform of St Andrews Priory, which is where the Catholic Congress was being held when Cormack's lot turned up. It was a terrifying experience.'

The wonder is that Jim Marin called these thugs 'gentlemen'. Despite this shameful spasm of sectarian violence, the Protestant Action councillors continued to serve on Edinburgh Corporation, a statement of widespread, and enduring, support. John Cormack was re-elected for another thirty years by the voters of South Leith, only retiring in 1963. He drove around the city in a van with 'No Popery' painted on it.

46

Almost a Capital

In the late Victorian period Edinburgh had industrialised and expanded, but the identity of the city appeared to drift. Having lost a parliament entirely, regained only temporary royal significance (at least once a year), and being the head-quarters of the Church of Scotland and the centre of the separate legal system, it retained some occasional sense of a capital city. But its dramatic setting, the dominant castle, and its stately and beautiful architecture all appeared to be a wonderful stage set for a play which was never performed. Power, real power, was not often to be found in provincial Edinburgh.

The government post of Scottish Secretary had been made a cabinet rank appointment in 1892, but the Scottish Office was in Dover House in London, not in Scotland. After the First World War, and the success of the nationalist movement in Ireland, the political weather began to change. In 1926 the Scottish Secretary became the Secretary of State for Scotland, and by 1939 his department had come to resemble a government in miniature with sub-departments of home affairs, agriculture, education and health. And in the same year the Scottish Office came home when St Andrew's House was opened on the southern flank of Calton Hill, on the site of the old jail.

It is one of the most beautiful buildings in Edinburgh, a masterpiece of 1930s architecture and design – and yet it is little visited. Influenced by the Art Deco movement, some of the interiors are opulent, especially the suite of offices for the Secretary of State. On the north-facing frontage superb sculpture surrounds the entrance with allegory and the appropriate motif of the Scottish thistle.

Despite the fact that its opening was submerged in the crises leading up to the outbreak of war in September 1939, this building and what it represented at last drew Edinburgh out of the drowsy nostalgia Scotland had dozed through in the previous hundred years. Power had returned – and more was to come.

When he became prime minister in 1940, Winston Churchill wisely appointed Labour Party MPs in his war cabinet to run the home ministries. There had been industrial unrest during the First World War, especially in Scotland, and politicians with links to the trade unions might be able to avoid problems. Churchill offered the job of Secretary of State for Scotland to a brilliant man, a genuine visionary, Tom Johnston. He refused at first, unless he was granted what amounted to vice-regal powers. He was, and Johnston used them. He created the Scottish Council of Industry, and it persuaded 700 companies, who employed more than 90,000 people, to relocate from England to Scotland. Committees were set up to deal with social issues like juvenile delinquency and also agricultural issues. Most influential was Johnston's creation of the Emergency Hospital Service. After the devastating Clydebank Blitz in 1941, when the town was devastated and many died or were injured, hospitals to deal with the casualties of more mass air raids were set up in rural locations, away from urban centres at places like Peel in the Scottish Borders, Raigmore near Inverness and Strathcathro in Angus. In the event, they were never used, and so Johnston, knowing that there were long wartime waiting lists, decreed that people should be treated free of charge. By the end of the war, 33,000 had passed through these new hospitals – and Johnston had showed the sceptics how a national health service might work.

Having established additional powers for the Secretary of State for Scotland, Tom Johnston had created a degree of devolution not seen since the departure of Scottish MPs to Westminster in 1707. By 1945 Edinburgh had almost become a capital city once more.

47

Festival City

After 1945, like the rest of Britain, Edinburgh found itself making do and mending in the austere aftermath. Following the sacrifices and tragedies of war, its cost continued to impoverish as war loans were paid off – it was not until 2006 that the last repayment was made to the USA. But in Edinburgh some light flickered in the grey skies of the 1940s. Rudolf Bing, who ran the Glyndebourne Festival Opera, wanted to see an arts festival founded in Britain after the war, something like the great classical music festivals he knew at Bayreuth and Salzburg. He met Harry Harvey Wood, Head of the British Council in Scotland. Wood left a record of what happened:

The Edinburgh International Festival of Music and Drama was first discussed over a lunch table in a restaurant in London, towards the end of 1944. Rudolf Bing, convinced that musical and operatic festivals on anything like the pre-war scale were unlikely to be held in any of the shattered and impoverished centres for many years to come, was anxious to consider and investigate the possibility of staging such a festival somewhere in the United Kingdom in the summer of 1946. He was convinced and he convinced my colleagues and myself that such an enterprise, successfully conducted, might at this moment of European time, be of more than temporary significance and might establish in Britain a centre of world resort for lovers of music, drama, opera, ballet and the graphic arts.

Certain preconditions were obviously required for such a centre. It should be a town of reasonable size, capable of absorbing and entertaining anything between 50,000 and 150,000 visitors over a three-week period to a month. It should, like Salzburg, have considerable scenic and picturesque appeal and it should be set in a country likely to be attractive to tourists and foreign visitors. It should have sufficient number of theatres, concert halls and open spaces for the adequate staging of a programme of an ambitious and varied character. Above all it should be a city likely to embrace the opportunity and willing to make the festival a major preoccupation not only in the City Chambers but in the heart and home of every citizen, however modest. Greatly daring but not without confidence I recommended Edinburgh as the centre and promised to make preliminary investigations.

Which Harry Harvey Wood did. Rudolf Bing came north to meet Edinburgh's Lord Provost, Sir William Falconer, who, to his undying credit, embraced the idea, put in a little municipal money and a great deal of encouragement. And it helped that, unlike London and other cities in the south, Edinburgh had remained largely intact.

The Edinburgh Festival was an immediate success. Rudolf Bing's excellent European contacts produced a first-rate classical music programme for the premiere in August 1947, a year later than planned. And the sun shone. Edinburgh basked in a glorious summer and crowds came out to the events in large numbers. The prior generosity of the brewer, Andrew Usher, enabled the Usher Hall to become the focal point for orchestral concerts and other recitals. Glamour, show business, opening nights, flashbulbs popping, divas and conductors, black tie and evening gowns – all of these lit the gloom of the post-war years in Edinburgh, and Scotland. And more than that, it did something magical and enduring. It is the only event in the calendar that shifts the cultural focus of Britain decisively away from London. And because it did that, Edinburgh's status as a political capital was buttressed by its becoming a cultural capital.

Something unexpected happened at the first festival in 1947, something that made the Edinburgh Festival absolutely unique and over the following decades would transform the city's image and make it a place of global significance. Eight theatre companies turned up to perform in the August of 1947. They were not in the official programme, and no one had invited them. Nevertheless, productions of *Macbeth*, *Murder in the Cathedral*, *The Anatomist* (about Dr Knox and Burke and Hare) and six other plays were mounted and drew healthy audiences. One critic called these groups Festival Adjuncts. More came in 1948 and, mercifully, the playwright Robert Kemp christened this phenomenon as the Festival Fringe. And it grew and grew.

By the early 1980s more than 500 groups had crammed into the city, and every performing art form was represented from comedy to dance to puppetry. Even bigger now, the Fringe has swamped the official festival, but in so doing it has brought the city alive in the summer. Using all of those church halls built after the Disruption, and many other spaces, it reaches all over Edinburgh, and since street theatre and music were finally permitted by a reluctant chief constable in the late 1970s, the colour and racket of celebration has spilled all over the central streets and open spaces. The crammed-together, cellular nature of the Old Town has nurtured the

Fringe, its old halls and meeting rooms being perfect for small-scale performance. The combined Edinburgh festivals (including the Book and Jazz & Blues festivals) are immensely lucrative, bringing in many millions of pounds, and they have also made Edinburgh internationally famous, the name a byword for innovation in the arts. As theatregoers rush past him to catch performances in the Assembly Hall on the Mound, John Knox appears no longer to thunder, but falls strangely silent, at last.

48

Edinburgh on the Edge

After the Second World War, the Festival was not the only radical innovation to affect the city. In 1949 urban planner Patrick Abercrombie promulgated a series of proposals which ultimately transformed Edinburgh – even though not all of them were carried through. Fundamental was the creation of large estates of public housing on the outskirts. These would relieve the overcrowding and poor living conditions in Gorgie, Dalry, Leith, Portobello, Pilrig and the Pleasance and also allow redevelopment once these rundown inner-city areas had been cleared. The New Jerusalem was promised. Houses with inside toilets, baths and efficient heating were quickly added to those built in the 1930s at Craigmillar, Piershill and Saughton. Vast new schemes went up at Drylaw, Muirhouse, Gilmerton, Oxgangs and Wester Hailes. Living conditions seemed at first a great improvement on the rickety, rat-infested, poorly serviced tenements of the Old Town and inner city. But two difficulties soon came to light. The need to build quickly, cheaply and in volume had in some places produced lower standards than the new residents either expected or deserved. Condensation, noise pollution and dampness affected many of the new flats and houses.

The planners had also failed to take sufficient account of what common amenities these new communities might need.

In the Old Town and its fringes, pubs, shops and small service businesses such as cobblers and repairers of other sorts had grown up with local demand and custom. Churches and church halls were still focal points. The Meadows and Bruntsfield Links were accessible to all. There were certainly some public parks in the new estates and small parades of shops, but mostly the ranks of grey-harled streets marched on unrelieved. And in such large communities, the informal mechanisms of social control which could operate well in tenements and closes were quickly overcome by those with little interest in thinking of their neighbours. By the 1970s many of the peripheral estates looked forlorn. Houses were sometimes simply abandoned and boarded up, particularly at ground-floor level, and the public spaces left to rot. A drug culture spread like a disease, and Edinburgh acquired an unwelcome reputation as shoot-up city.

For the historic centre, Abercrombie and his supporters planned aggressively modern development. Fifty years before, Patrick Geddes had also wished to see changes, in the Old Town in particular, but his views were different. He had the house of Allan Ramsay, the artist, extended and remodelled. In what came to be called Ramsay Garden, rooms for Edinburgh University students and private flats were built in the 1890s. The result is magnificent, an organic development clinging to the edge of Castlehill and the Esplanade, entirely in keeping with the Old Town and a highly visible adornment to the city. What Edinburgh University planned in the 1950s and the 1960s was to be far from sympathetic and certainly far from an adornment.

The core idea was straightforward enough and could have been appealing. As the tumbledown rookeries of the Southside decanted their residents to the outlying estates, Edinburgh University would be encouraged to create an academic enclave centred on George Square, Old College, the McEwan Hall, the Reid School of Music and the Medical Faculty next to the Royal Infirmary. But the planners planned to be ruthless. Much of George Square, the earliest example of Georgian town planning in the city, was demolished to make way for undistinguished modern towers, with no ivory to be seen, and the well-designed new university library. North of George Square, the Parker's Triangle was entirely effaced and replaced by a temporary car park. Bounded by Charles Street, Potterow and Crichton Street, the Triangle was named after Parker's Stores, an excellent emporium selling goods at discount prices. Charles Street was particularly notable with well-set Georgian tenements and the Paperback Bookshop. It housed performances during the Festival Fringe and its management helped create the Traverse Theatre in 1962, a permanent legacy of the festival. Just as Edinburgh University succeeded in having all of these homely and interesting streets erased, it appeared to run out of the money needed for the building projects planned for the site. The temporary car park remained in place for a disgraceful forty years.

Elsewhere the developers at least managed to replace what they had destroyed. Notably, the brutalist St James Centre, a shopping mall, was planted on the site of St James' Square, Georgian housing to the east of St Andrew Square. It too fell victim to the wrecking ball and was replaced by the much lighter and more user-friendly St James Quarter. It has some excellent restaurants and a good retail offering. Controversially, the entire edifice is topped by something that looks to older observers like a Walnut Whip.

Irony took a hand when the demolition crews dumped the rubble of Georgian St James Square into Craigleith Quarry. Much of the stone for the New Town had come out of it in the late eighteenth and early nineteenth centuries.

The greatest threat from so-called modernisers was the project known as the Inner Ring Road. As it tunnelled under the Old Town and roared through the Meadows, it would have devastated much of the historic city. Conservationists finally rallied and rose up against the scheme, and after a public enquiry in 1967, it was abandoned, and common sense returned.

49

Reconvened

As often throughout the city's long history, politics began once more to stir and reshape Edinburgh. In the 1970s the Scottish National Party broke through into the mainstream and forced the Labour and Conservative parties at least to have policies rather than attitudes to home rule. Labour had become the political establishment in Scotland (even douce Edinburgh had a Labour lord provost), and in order to contain the Scottish National Party as well as meet the wishes and expectations of their own supporters, the Callaghan government agreed to a referendum in 1979. Yes and No campaigns debated vigorously, but the intervention of a London MP proved determinant. A simple majority in favour of constitutional change would not be enough; at least 40 per cent of the electorate had to vote Yes for there to be what was then called a Scottish Assembly. Despite this, the portents were favourable, and the old Royal High School building (the RHS had decamped to a new site in Barnton in the west of the city) was converted into a debating chamber and offices. It lay handily near St Andrew's House.

It was not to be needed. When the results came in, they showed a majority in favour of devolution for Scotland, but it fell short of the 40 per cent required, and the proposed bill therefore fell. Edinburgh would not have a new parliament after all, and the debating chamber gathered dust, empty and unused.

Almost immediately the mood appeared to change. While Scotland voted mostly Labour in successive general elections, England chose the Conservatives and, as prime minister, Margaret Thatcher. Instead of withering after the disappointments of 1979, support for Scottish devolution began to harden, much encouraged by what came to be known as 'The Sermon on the Mound'. In 1988 the General Assembly of the Church of Scotland invited Mrs Thatcher to give an address. She announced that the Church existed to promote personal redemption and not social reform and that, incidentally, there was no such thing as community. These contentious views, and her quote from 'I Vow to Thee My Country' (a hymn not included in the Scottish hymnary), were greeted by a polite scatter of applause from ministers and elders. Mrs Thatcher was then thanked by the moderator, the Reverend Professor James Whyte. Without a flicker, he gave the prime minister two pamphlets which he hoped might interest her. One was concerned with justice, fairness and poverty in society and the other dealt with issues relating to public housing. He also remarked that he thought it unlikely that Mrs Thatcher had ever been in the company of so many people who had prayed for her.

Despite Margaret Thatcher's polarising unpopularity in Scotland, devolution and a parliament would take another ten years to come. It required the landslide Labour victory of 1997 and a majority in a subsequent referendum for the Scottish Parliament to reconvene at last in 1999. Yet more irony unfolded as temporary premises were found in the Assembly Hall on the Mound. MSPs (Members of the Scottish Parliament) were elected, trooped past Knox's statue and took their places in the chamber. It was only appropriate, for the Church of Scotland and its annual assembly had remained a bastion of Scottishness for the three centuries when there was no parliament in Edinburgh.

In the first elections the Labour Party gained the largest number of seats, but not an overall majority, and formed a coalition with the Liberals. Donald Dewar became first minister. It seemed that a new politics and a new beginning was at hand, but instead the entire project became immediately mired in a controversy which threatened to distract, even derail, the devolution settlement in its infancy.

In 1998 Holyrood had been chosen as the most appropriate place for the new parliament building and not the old Royal High School at Calton Hill. Soon after the rejection of devolution in 1979 a vigil began at the gates of the old school, and it may have been that the building was too closely identified with the Scottish National Party and the controversies of the past. Scottish Labour politicians in particular argued that the accommodation was outdated, the rooms too restricted and too small. The fact that the old Royal High lay very close to St Andrew's House seemed not to matter at all. And so Scottish & Newcastle breweries sold their site at Holyrood, moved out and work began on demolition.

Meanwhile an architectural competition was advertised to find the right design. Enric Miralles, a Catalonian architect, won, and his very different, very bold concept went on display. Costs began quickly to spiral and became the cause of justifiable outrage as they climbed towards an astonishing £414 million.

For £414 million Edinburgh and Scotland bought a strange piece of architecture, not particularly Scottish in feel. The exterior appears both cluttered and fussy as well as oddly arranged and difficult to read. But the debating chamber is nothing short of a triumph, a beautifully handled space that impresses yet does not overawe. Grey concrete is the primary and very dull finish, but here and there wood, metal and stone enliven.

The impact of the fact of the parliament on Edinburgh has nevertheless been electric. Not only has the Canongate and Holyrood bloomed into life as media outlets cluster and new hotels are opened, but also the Edinburgh economy is booming. Power attracts business and business brings investment. Edinburgh feels like a capital city, dynamic and adaptable. The new hotels buzz with conferences and the meetings of busy people anxious to work close to the new parliament and its politicians and civil servants. And the great city supplies a rich setting for all of that bustle and hustle, making the centuries between 1707 and 1999 seem like a hiatus. At the outset of the twenty-first century Edinburgh is Edinburgh again.

50

The Tenth Century

Guarded by the protective shadow of the castle, Edinburgh's skyline is punctuated by spires. Near the top of the Royal Mile, the Highland Tolbooth Church reached for the vaults of Heaven, the echoes of the psalms once sung there by its Gaelic-speaking congregations swirling in the sea wind. The majestic vista along Princes Street is completed by the three spires of St Mary's Episcopal Cathedral, and at the head of Leith Walk, the stained glass of the façade of St Mary's Catholic Cathedral glows as it looks down to the harbours and the North Sea beyond. Glowering over the gardens and the shoppers on Princes Street are the dour, spiky twin towers of the Assembly Hall, where the General Assembly of the Church of Scotland gathers in May of every year. Simply by looking around the city, in every direction, a casual observer might conclude that Edinburgh was a place of great piety, where churches might welcome the faithful in their brimming thousands.

In fact, what they are looking at is archaeology, the remains of once powerful, pervasive, defining institutions. In 1957 the Church of Scotland had 1,320,000 members, about 27 per cent of the population of the whole country. But in the span of little more than two generations, those numbers have collapsed, spectacularly. By 2022, there were only 283,600 members, but the vast majority of those never went to church on a Sunday morning. Estimates vary, but they all hover around a weekly attendance of 60,000 – in the whole of Scotland. Precise figures are difficult to find, especially in the wake of the COVID pandemic of 2020/21, but on the basis of population size it seems reasonable to assume that perhaps only 6,000 make up all the congregations of the Kirk in Edinburgh. Parishes are amalgamating everywhere as numbers shrivel and ministers retire. And it is certain that in the coming decade, many Edinburgh churches will close and be sold off. The Highland Tolbooth has been renamed The Hub and is the headquarters of the Edinburgh International Festival. Land values are high in the city, and money is always needed by the Kirk. Many of these old churches, places where generations were baptised, married and buried, will probably be demolished, and history erased. This radical change will affect many more than churchgoers. The groups who use their church halls, the likes of lunch clubs, playgroups, badminton players, scouts and guides and many other community organisations will find themselves homeless, unable to afford alternatives.

The Catholic Church is also in steep decline, although its total numbers are likely to be much higher than in the Kirk. In 2011 there were 841,053 Catholics in Scotland, and when more recent figures become available, there is likely to have been decline. The scandals associated with the former Archbishop of Edinburgh, Cardinal Keith O'Brien, as well as a litany of child abuse will have almost certainly turned people away.

There are four mosques in Edinburgh and all seem well supported. The Central Mosque in Potterow is an imposing building with a tall minaret to add to the spires on the skyline, and its plain but beautifully proportioned interior speaks of a different sanctity. Prayers can be heard six times a day, beginning with a bracingly early session known as Fajr from around 3 a.m. until 4 a.m. It is estimated that around 15,000 Muslims live in Edinburgh. Most originated in southern Asia, and there is also a significant contingent from Pakistan. To make attendance at daily prayers more convenient, there are a dozen or so prayer rooms in various parts of the city.

By the outset of the twenty-first century, the Jewish community in Edinburgh had shrunk. Two memories of when it was much larger are to be found close to each other. In Salisbury Place on the south side of the city there is an active synagogue, and in nearby Sciennes House Place, a Jewish cemetery that was established in 1816.

While God seems to be in retreat, Mammon has made significant advances. Edinburgh is now very prosperous and has the most vibrant economy of any city in Britain except for London. This is not an impression or an assertion, but the result of precise measurement. After London, the city has the second highest rating of GVA, Gross Value Added for each resident, that is, the monetary value of all the goods and services produced in Edinburgh. Average gross annual earnings by each resident is also ranked second in Britain, and the number claiming Jobseeker's Allowance in 2012 was 3.2 per cent, the lowest in Britain. There are clearly jobs to be had in Edinburgh, and the population is increasing as more and more people are attracted by the strong local economy. In the 2001 Census, 448,600 lived in the city; by 2011 that had risen to 476,600. The numbers given in the 2021 Census are less reliable (because of a historically low rate of returned forms), but it is generally agreed that the population of Edinburgh leapt up by 10 per cent in ten years to a high of 526,470. Especially obvious in the south of the city, new house building seems to be springing up in many places to meet demand. Edinburgh is more prosperous than ever before.

There can be no doubt that the opening of the Scottish Parliament in 1999 has been a major stimulus for all this growth, giving it real and continuing momentum. Propinquity to power matters. Edinburgh has once again become a capital city, and any company ambitious to do significant business in Scotland requires a presence in the city. Also, the business of government itself has created jobs: the Scottish government employs more than 4,000 people.

One of the concrete symbols of Edinburgh's twenty-first-century prosperity has been the creation of the new financial district in the West End. Much of it stands on the site of the old Princes Street Railway Station that used to operate behind the Waldorf Astoria (formerly the Caledonian) Hotel. Masterminded by the eminent architect, Sir Terry Farrell, an extensive area of offices in Exchange Crescent and Exchange Plaza has been built in the last three decades. He also designed the Edinburgh International Conference Centre on Morrison Street. When the Scottish Parliament was using the Assembly Hall before it moved to Holyrood, the General Assembly of the Church of Scotland met there, an unlikely setting. More than twenty companies have their offices in the new buildings, including Lloyd's Banking Group, abrdn plc, Scottish Widows, IBM, KPMG and others. And on the western edge of Edinburgh more big companies are to be found. The Tesco Bank has its headquarters at South Gyle and employs 2,400 people. Before its spectacular and deeply damaging fall from grace in 2008, the Royal Bank of Scotland had built a new headquarters at Gogarburn, not far from the airport. Edinburgh is reckoned to be the thirteenth largest financial centre in the world and the fourth largest in Europe.

The city's economy is fuelled from another, very different source. Stories bring millions of visitors to Edinburgh each year. The story of the city, its history and its great beauty, the astonishing flowering of festivals in August when it becomes the arts capital of the world, telling thousands of tales, and also the work of great writers, dead and living, make Edinburgh the second most visited city in Britain. Each year, all year round, and not just in the summer, approximately 4 million people come, and they contribute a huge £1.2 billion to the local economy.

And it is stories that bring them north, those of the past, and Edinburgh's unique architecture, the contrast of the Old Town with the New Town, the everyday drama of what Robert Louis Stevenson called his 'precipitous city'. Visitors come to many places to go to 'attractions', to theatres, concerts, galleries, exhibitions, sporting events and other activities. They come to Edinburgh for those reasons, but also to look at it, to walk around the streets, to move through history, to look up at the grand buildings, 75 per cent of them listed in the centre, far more than anywhere else, to look out to the Forth, and to the Pentlands and the Lammermuirs to the south. They inhabit what instinct tells them is a living masterpiece, a very different world from the everyday. To say of Edinburgh that it is beautiful seems not to be enough, and yet it is everything.

From Sir Walter Scott's 'mine own romantic town' onwards, writers have attached many adjectives and apercus to what visitors gaze at. But in the twenty-first century, the city has been blessed and chronicled by several internationally famous novelists, the sales of whose work run into many tens of millions of copies. Ian Rankin's Inspector Rebus series speaks sometimes of the darker side of the city, as did Irvine Welsh's novel of its drug culture, *Trainspotting*. But perhaps the writer who most consistently captures the essence of life in Edinburgh is Alexander McCall Smith.

In his series of novels featuring Isabel Dalhousie, who lives in the south of the city, near Bruntsfield Links, and the community in the tenement flats in 44 Scotland Street in the

New Town, reality and fiction are often blurred. McCall Smith recognises that a dominant character in the novels is the city itself as stories seem to come up through the cobbles and out of the walls. And the fabric of the city is like a palimpsest of history and fiction with the ever-presence of writers baked into its core. Around the corner from Big Lou's café used by the characters from the 44 Scotland Street series is the house in Heriot Row where Robert Louis Stevenson sat at his bedroom window waiting for the leerie to light his lamp. Somehow Edinburgh seems to speak many languages to its residents and visitors, but perhaps it is most fluent in one language above all others, and that is the language of love. The last words in this brief history of the city should go to Alexander McCall Smith, perhaps the man who is most fluent in that language:

> Fact and fiction meet in this city all the time. And why not? Edinburgh is a place in which the imagination seems to thrive. There is something in the air here, something in the light. I'm not sure exactly what it is, but it's there. Edinburgh has been called a dream in stone. Perhaps that explains it.

51

Envoi

The fact that Edinburgh is the most beautiful city in the world is not only a matter of subjective judgement; it is also demonstrable. Geology, architecture, history and accident all combine to make it unique, a combination of characteristics found nowhere else.

Many cities are built on the banks of wide rivers, like London and Paris, and that usually means a flat site where buildings, streets and public spaces dominate. While many are very beautiful and impressive, there is often a powerful sense of enclosure, with few long vistas, apart from the riverbanks. Because it is built on steep hills and ridges, Edinburgh is different and easy to see out of, to see the city in its setting. And there are two quite different aspects to be enjoyed. From many not particularly elevated places, such as the junction of George Street and Hanover Street, there are very pleasing views of the sea, the Firth of Forth, the Fife coastal towns and the hills beyond. To the south rise the green heads of the Pentland and Lammermuir Hills, a particular memory of Robert Louis Stevenson in exile in the South Pacific. These are everyday sights, but for those who walk up to the castle and the esplanade the views are breathtaking, leading the eye away into the distance on every side.

Inside the city there is more drama. Geology carved out the canyon of the Cowgate, and from George IV Bridge and

South Bridge the descent is dizzying. On the northern flanks of the High Street, the sharp fall of the ground makes buildings like the Bank of Scotland Head Office and the Assembly Hall appear impossibly monumental, taller than they really are. The long incline of Leith Walk leads to the port and the sea beyond. From the suburbs it is almost always possible to see the Castle Rock and the centre of the city – making it difficult to feel lost.

Edinburgh is not large, or anonymous, or hemmed in. Despite the expansion triggered by the presence of the Scottish Parliament, the population of half a million or so seems comfortable. Enough to justify everything a city might have to offer but not too large to prevent enjoyment of galleries, theatres, sporting arenas, cinemas – even during the festival the pavements are manageable and public spaces allow relief from the press of the crowds.

Perhaps the best place to see it, to consider and enjoy the character of the beautiful city and watch it bustle is also one of the most frequented. From Calton Hill, sitting on the base of Edinburgh's Disgrace, it is possible to gaze at many of Edinburgh's glories. On a summer evening, the western view along Princes Street is eloquent. Edinburgh lies below in all its richness, all its vitality and all its ancient beauty.

In January 1976, I began a lifelong love affair with the city. The board of the Festival Fringe Society took a considerable risk when they hired a twenty-five-year-old with little experience of anything much to run what was soon to become the largest arts festival in the world. So many performers wanted to come, I had to scour Edinburgh for more and more spaces, large and small. I explored every close and wynd off the Royal Mile, every church hall and school hall, all the masonic lodges, and the accommodation owned by the universities and colleges. I walked everywhere, knocked on doors and made hundreds of phone calls. I even went up to the Castle Esplanade with binoculars to scan the city, looking for big roofs. Very quickly, I came to know Edinburgh intimately, and not just the centre. Fringe groups performed in the suburbs, in Leith, Portobello, even Musselburgh.

Any visitor or native can enjoy the daily drama of the great vistas of the precipitous city, but what I discovered was its detail, its hidden richness, the marks left on Edinburgh by generations of its inhabitants. There are unlikely gems around many corners, like the Lodge Canongate Kilwinning, built in the eighteenth century, or its near neighbour in the Old Town, St Patrick's Church, in all its symmetrical classical splendour. There are dozens of other beautiful buildings and features to be found and enjoyed for their character and often their quirkiness.

What also drew me close was perhaps Edinburgh's greatest asset, its greatest treasure, and that was (almost) all the people I met and dealt with in my time running the Fringe. Contrary to the cliché, residents enjoy the Festival, and particularly the Fringe, and I found support wherever I looked, from the city's famously conservative legal establishment to the ministers with good church halls and head teachers with facilities for hire. Even the police, after a shaky start, were helpful when we persuaded them to allow street theatre and busking. When they agreed to the first closure of the High Street between George IV and South Bridges, Edinburgh seemed to come alive as people gathered to watch outdoor performances.

The city seemed to me then to be a genuine community, with working links that usually led to positive conclusions. And I think that is to do with scale. Edinburgh is not a huge conurbation, but smaller and more intimate, a legacy perhaps from David I's 143 acres, certainly something encouraged by geography. The city also attracts great loyalty. Its citizens are proud of Edinburgh, and they care about its fabric and its services. Each August, the gigantic party known as the Edinburgh Festival allows them not only to enjoy the talents of all the performers who come, but also to celebrate the city that hosts them – their city, their own romantic town.

That is what you have in your hands – a celebration, a unique story of a remarkable place, the most beautiful city in the world.

Further Reading

Buchan, James, *Capital of the Mind: How Edinburgh Changed the World*, Edinburgh, 2007

Coghill, Hamish, *Lost Edinburgh: Edinburgh's Lost Architectural Heritage*, Edinburgh, 2008

Cosh, Mary, *Edinburgh: The Golden Age*, Edinburgh, 2014

Daiches, David, *Edinburgh*, London, 1978

Edwards, Owen Dudley, *Burke and Hare*, Edinburgh: 2014

Fleet, Christopher and MacCannell, Daniell, *Edinburgh: Mapping the City*, Edinburgh, 2014

Fry, Michael, *Edinburgh: A History of the City*, London, 2010

Harris, Stuart, *The Place Names of Edinburgh: Their Origins and History*, Edinburgh, 1996

Herman, Arthur, *The Scottish Enlightenment: The Scots' Invention of the Modern World*, London, 2003

Keay, John & Keay, Julia, *Collins Encyclopaedia of Scotland*, London, 2000.

Massie, Allan, *Edinburgh*, Edinburgh, 1995

McCall Smith, Alexander, *A Work of Beauty: Alexander McCall Smith's Edinburgh*, Edinburgh, 2016

McKirdy, Alan, *Edinburgh: Landscapes in Stone*, Edinburgh, 2017

McWilliam, Colin, Gifford, John & Walker, David, *Edinburgh: The Buildings of Scotland*, London: 1984

Smith, Charles J., *Historic South Edinburgh*, Edinburgh, 2023

Szatkowski, Sheila, *Enlightenment Edinburgh: A Guide*, Edinburgh, 2017

Taylor, Alan (ed.), *Edinburgh: The Autobiography*, Edinburgh, 2024

Index

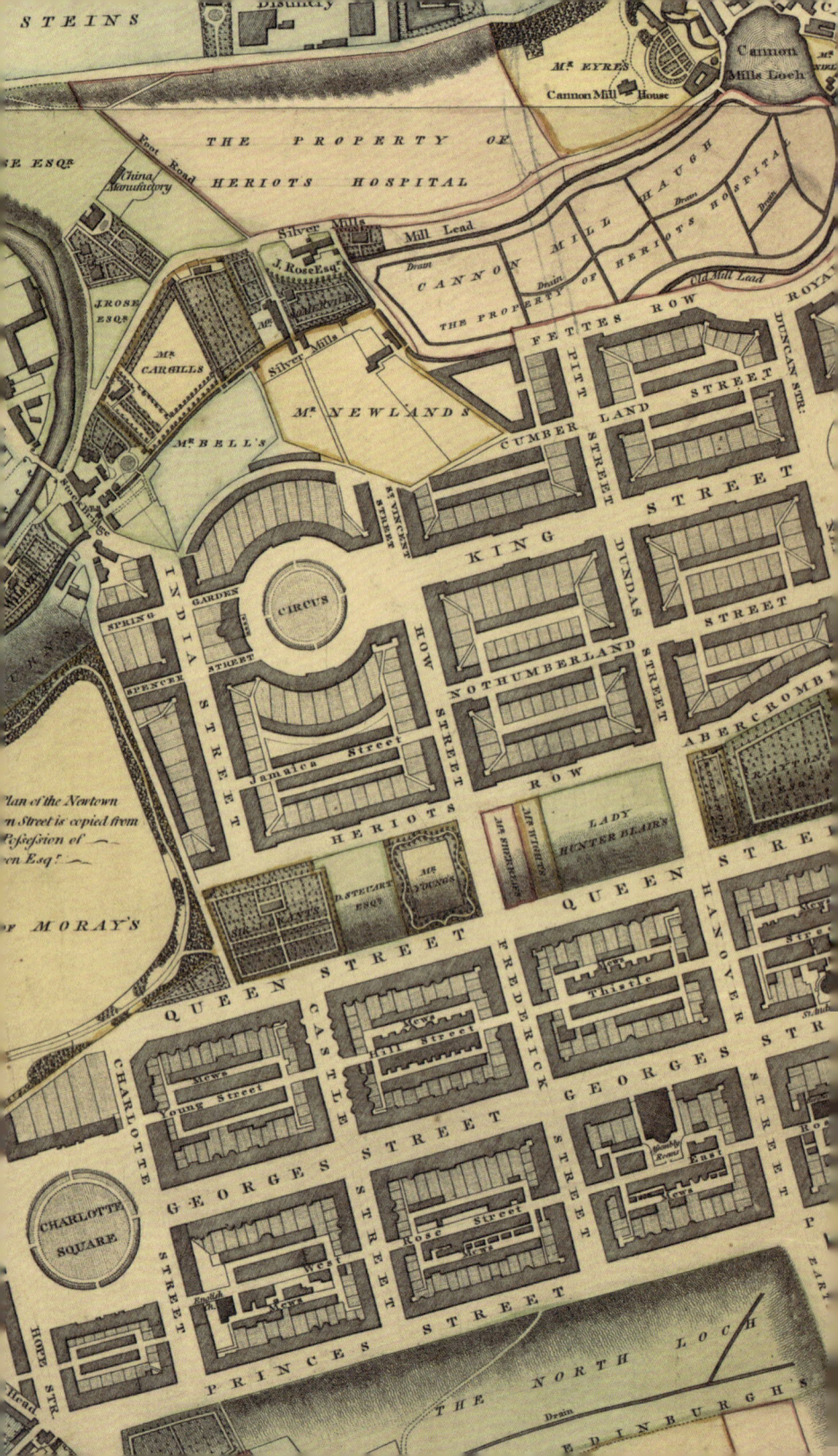